PRAISE FOR
THE SMART
BRANDING BOOK

FOR OTHER TITLES
IN THE SERIES...

CONCISE
ADVICE
LAB

SMALL BOOKS: BIG IDEAS

CLEVER CONTENT, DYNAMIC IDEAS, PRACTICAL
SOLUTIONS AND ENGAGING VISUALS –
A CATALYST TO INSPIRE NEW WAYS OF THINKING
AND PROBLEM-SOLVING IN A COMPLEX WORLD

www.lidpublishing.com/product-category/concise-advice-series

Published by
LID Publishing
An imprint of LID Business Media Ltd.
LABS House, 15-19 Bloomsbury Way,
London, WC1A 2TH, UK

info@lidpublishing.com
www.lidpublishing.com

A member of:

BPR ⊛
businesspublishersroundtable.com

© Dan White, 2023
© LID Business Media Limited, 2023
Reprinted in 2024

Printed and bound in Great Britain by Halstan Ltd

ISBN: 978-1-911687-70-2
ISBN: 978-1-911687-71-9 (ebook)

Cover and page design: Caroline Li

THE SMART BRANDING BOOK

HOW TO BUILD A PROFITABLE AND RESILIENT BRAND

DAN WHITE

MADRID | MEXICO CITY | LONDON
BUENOS AIRES | BOGOTA | SHANGHAI

CONTENTS

INTRODUCTION

A company's long-term commercial success relies on it delivering products or services that live up to customers' expectations. This drives repeat purchasing. In any competitive market, however, a growth strategy based on product superiority is unsustainable. Innovations are soon copied since patents only offer limited protection. Competitors can launch 'me-too' products without high research and development costs. This makes brand-building a necessary tool to drive growth and profit while making the brand more resilient to competitive threats.

The concept of a brand is straightforward. It is something potential customers recognize and that conjures a set of mental associations. Powerful, positive associations make people more likely to buy the product, while negative associations may drive them away. However, building a successful brand is not simple. It delivers large commercial rewards but requires money, creativity and patience. *The Smart Branding Book* is for anyone looking to understand why brand-building is a sound investment as well as how to conceive, nurture and get the most from a brand.

Chapter 1 explains the origins of branding and the various ways it can help a business. *Chapter 2* provides guidance on deciding what your brand should represent and how to plan for growth. *Chapters 3* and *4* describe the brand-building process and the roles of "distinctive brand assets" (Romaniuk, 2018), innovation and communications. The value of creativity, originality and consistency within marketing is discussed in *Chapter 5*, and *Chapter 6* explores how different media channels can be used most effectively to build brands. *Chapter 7* outlines how to measure brand perceptions, determine brands' value and track progress against a brand's objectives.

Over a career spanning 30 years, the author has built an encyclopaedic knowledge of brand-building. He was one of the architects of Kantar BrandZ, the world's leading brand equity development system, and is a thought leader in marketing communications and the author of the bestselling *The Smart Marketing Book* (White, 2020). His unique frameworks and illustrations have received widespread acclaim within the marketing community and are used by lecturers throughout the world. *The Smart Branding Book* is based in this expertise and the author's passionate belief in the value of brands. Given the contribution brands make to commercial success, marketers should all understand the principles and practices of brand-building. *The Smart Branding Book* is their indispensable guide.

CHAPTER 1

PROVE
OWNERSHIP

ENABLE
ACCOUNTABILITY

PROVIDE
WARNING

INFORM
ADMIRERS

BUILD
FAMILIARITY

GUARANTEE
AUTHENTICITY

WHY
BRANDING
EXISTS

THE ORIGINS OF BRANDING

The word 'brand' originally meant 'to permanently mark with a flame.' It came to mean 'distinctive marking' in the 15th century, when farmers started using hot irons to burn symbols onto their property to show ownership.

Branding has performed a variety of roles over the centuries.

PURPOSES OF BRANDING

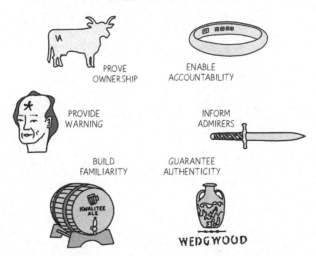

PROVE OWNERSHIP

ENABLE ACCOUNTABILITY

PROVIDE WARNING

INFORM ADMIRERS

BUILD FAMILIARITY

GUARANTEE AUTHENTICITY

KWALITEE ALE

WEDGWOOD

PROVE OWNERSHIP

According to Karl Moore and Susan Reid (2008), the use of branding is as old as civilization itself. Cave paintings show animals with symbols on their hinds. To this day, farmers brand their livestock to prove which animals they own and deter thieves. Likewise, brand owners use trademarks to indicate ownership of brand names, and logos and patents to prevent competitors from stealing their inventions.

ENABLE ACCOUNTABILITY

The stone masons in ancient Egypt engraved a symbol on the stones they cut for the Great Pyramids so that they would be paid a fair amount. The contractor would use the symbols to keep tally of the stones used in the construction and pay each supplier accordingly. To this day, goldsmiths are required to stamp hallmarks on their work to identify them and certify the purity of the metal so that unscrupulous practitioners can be called to account.

INFORM ADMIRERS

For centuries, artisans have put identifying symbols on their work. This meant that potential customers who had seen and admired their well-crafted products would know where to take their custom. Designer brands do the same today. Many of Gucci's products proudly feature its interlocking double-G logo, the initials of the company's founder, Guccio Gucci. Every Nike shoe proudly shows the brand's famous 'swoosh.'

GUARANTEE AUTHENTICITY

Wedgwood, the porcelain manufacturer, used the logo replicated in the drawing above in the mid-18th century to help buyers identify genuine Wedgwood items. For 5,000 years, makers of fine pottery in China also marked their pieces to assure potential buyers of their provenance and quality. Branding of this sort helps customers to identify quality products and avoid potentially inferior imitations. The same challenge exists today. Kellogg's produces high-quality breakfast cereals, but its products are widely copied and the quality of these alternative products is often inferior. For decades, Kellogg's has used the phrase "If it doesn't say Kellogg's on the box, it isn't Kellogg's in the box" to encourage consumers to consider whether copy-cat products are as good as those made by Kellogg's.

BUILD FAMILIARITY

During the Industrial Revolution, when mass-produced goods first became available, consumers were suspicious of generic products from distant factories. They favoured the local products they had trusted for years. To overcome this, the factories started to put brand names on their supply crates and barrels, to build a sense of familiarity and appeal. This was later extended to individual products. Building brand familiarity has become one of the most important concepts in modern marketing.

PROVIDE WARNING

The phrase 'branded a criminal' refers to the practice of permanently marking criminals on the skin with burns or tattoos to make them instantly recognizable. Modern marketers, watch out – if your brand gains a poor reputation, there's no going back.

Branding can play any of these roles in marketing today. Marketers need to identify which are most relevant to their circumstances and develop their brand accordingly. Note that in all cases, branding involves making a product easy to distinguish from others. High-quality brands have plenty to gain from doing this. Products with a bad reputation may need to change their identity.

1.2 WHAT IS BRANDING?

A brand can mean different things to different people, but here's a definition that's useful to marketers:

A BRAND CONSISTS OF ALL THE ...

mental connections & responses

people have to a brand's name.

In other words, a brand is whatever is in the mind of the target audience. Marketers can write a description of what they want the brand to be, but that's only an aspiration. Whether it becomes a reality depends on what people experience when they buy and use the brand or encounter communications about it (see *Section 4.1*).

A brand is like anything else stored in human memory. It's a set of ideas that have become connected together in the mind and the feelings generated by these ideas. Connections form between ideas if they repeatedly come to mind at the same time.

Tulving and Donaldson (1972) described how humans have three memory systems.

THE THREE MEMORY SYSTEMS

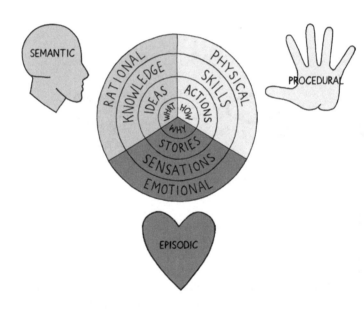

Semantic memories relate to our rational understanding. They are our knowledge and beliefs. For a brand, these include what it's called, what it does, its functional benefits and its supporting claims.

Episodic memories provide social and emotional understanding. They are captured via images, symbols and stories – and any feelings they evoke.

Procedural memories are about our physical understanding. How the brand is experienced, including any rituals (see *Section 3.2*), is stored in this system.

Memories that include multiple systems are more powerful and long-lasting. Brands should leverage a variety of experiences, channels and messages to build memories in all three systems.

Here's what a brand can look like in someone's mind. This depiction is for the British TV series *Life on Mars*, named after the David Bowie track. The question marks at the centre of the image represent how, while creating the image, the author remembered a lot about the series but couldn't remember its name.

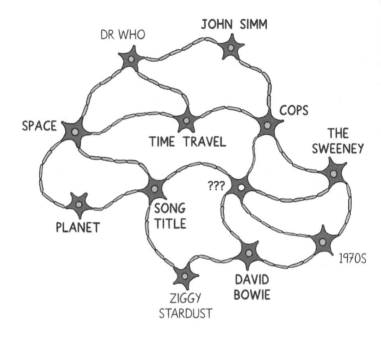

This illustrates that although a brand's name is an important component, it is one of many elements. Brands are made up of words, sounds, images and concepts.

If this defines a brand, what is branding?

Branding refers to the efforts a company makes to shape consumer perceptions to make its products more likely to be bought at the asking price.

1.3 HOW BRANDS GROW

In theory, there are four ways to grow your brand:
* Get more people to buy it
* Charge more for it
* Get existing buyers to buy it more often
* Retain more customers than previously

In practice, long-term growth almost always comes from getting more people to buy your brand (Ehrenberg, 1969). In *How Brands Grow* (2010), Byron Sharp describes the extensive scientific evidence that supports this. A brand's market share is closely related to its penetration (e.g. the number of people who buy it in 12 months). Brand loyalty (e.g. the average number of times buyers buy the brand in 12 months) doesn't vary much between brands and can be predicted accurately based on brand penetration. Ehrenberg and Sharp refer to the strong connection between penetration and loyalty as "Double Jeopardy."

DOUBLE-JEOPARDY EXAMPLE
(US SHAMPOOS, 2005)

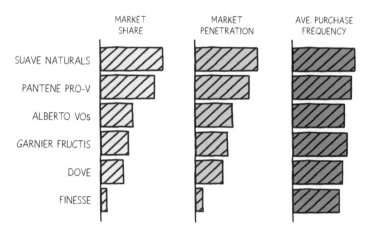

The Double Jeopardy law applies to business-to-consumer and business-to-business brands across all categories.

So, growing penetration is essential for brand growth. Marketers, therefore, need to:
- Focus on continually bringing in new customers
- Deliver a good product to avoid excessive customer defection
- Produce advertising that's relevant to potential future buyers as well as current ones
- Choose media that will reach a broad cross-section of category buyers rather than a niche

It also means that marketing activities designed mainly for existing customers are unlikely to help grow your brand. Examples include advertising seen only by existing customers and loyalty programmes. These marketing activities may play a role in the mix but only if they do not absorb significant time and resources.

So the goal is to get more and more people to buy the brand. The role of marketing is to marshal the company's resources to maximize the number of people who start buying the brand while ensuring existing customers continue to buy. This is achieved through brand-building. Here's a visual summary of how it works.

HOW BRAND-BUILDING WORKS

When people come across a brand, a whole load of **ASSOCIATIONS** come to mind.

... or if someone wants or **NEEDS** something, the brand and its associations spring to mind ...

Associations are built up whenever the brand is brought to people's mind e.g. when **EXPERIENCING** advertising or the product itself

The better the **STRATEGY** the more effective the associations will be at making the brand feel like the right choice

... making the brand feel like **THE RIGHT CHOICE** instinctively, so people are more likely to choose it and pay the asking price

For a well-managed brand, the **ROI** from brand-building initiatives is high

The three central sentences describe what Byron Sharp calls "mental availability," which is created and maintained through brand-building. Brands grow if they are mentally available and physically available – i.e. quick and easy to buy where and when consumers want to buy the category.

Done right, brand-building is worth every penny. *The Smart Branding Book* exists to equip marketers with the knowledge and inspiration to build profitable, long-lasting brands that people welcome into their lives.

1.4 BRANDING ALONG THE PATH TO PURCHASE

Marketers can tip the balance in their brand's favour through branding activity. The benefit of strong branding occurs at every stage of the path to purchase. The Lazy Sales River is a way of visualizing the journey.

THE LAZY SALES RIVER

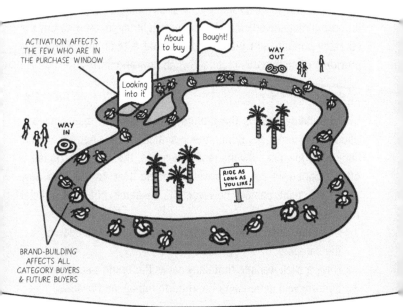

ACTIVATION AFFECTS THE FEW WHO ARE IN THE PURCHASE WINDOW

About to buy

Bought!

WAY OUT

Looking into it

WAY IN

RIDE AS LONG AS YOU LIKE!

BRAND-BUILDING AFFECTS ALL CATEGORY BUYERS & FUTURE BUYERS

FUTURE CATEGORY BUYERS

People start and stop buying a product category at any time – for example, as their life stage or needs change. When people enter the category (or get on the 'ride'), they might have a particular brand in mind. This is usually a brand they are highly familiar with due to brand-building advertising or word of mouth they have experienced. Brands that people are favourably disposed to when they enter the category have a major advantage.

CATEGORY BUYERS WHO ARE NOT READY TO BUY AGAIN

People already in the market spend most of their time disinterested in it. They don't typically seek information about it – especially if they are happy with the brand they previously bought. People at this point in the cycle can still be influenced, however. Another brand could become more prominent in their mind through consistent brand-building advertising. Or a brand might trigger them to buy the category sooner than planned by offering a tempting deal. Utility providers often use this tactic ("Switch now and save").

PEOPLE LOOKING INTO BUYING THE CATEGORY

Brand-building shapes the brands people have in their consideration set. Experiences during the 'research' phase shape their final choice. In low-risk, low-interest categories, the research phase is often skipped. In categories where people need to feel they have made the right choice, however, the research phase is crucial. Brands should aim to:

- Dominate search results for terms people use to research the category
- Have a slick website that showcases the brand's superiority
- Perform well in consumer and trade ratings and reviews

Even if a person doesn't know a brand beforehand, a strong showing during the research phase can make sure it gets onto the list of contenders.

PEOPLE ABOUT TO BUY THE CATEGORY

When people are in the about to buy category, they usually have one or a few brands they'd be happy with. If your brand is one of them, you need to minimize the chance that the customer will be diverted from buying you. Make it as quick and easy to buy as possible. Be available widely. Avoid being out of stock. Leverage e-commerce. If your brand isn't many people's top choice yet, grab their attention at the point of sale. Offer a tempting deal or an extended warranty – anything that might tip the odds in your favour.

PEOPLE WHO BOUGHT YOUR BRAND LAST TIME

What customers experience once they've bought a brand is also important – how easy they found it to access customer support, for example, and how quickly their problem was resolved. These after-sales experiences have a big impact on brand perceptions, influencing the chances of repeat purchasing. They also determine whether a buyer becomes an advocate (helping to attract new buyers) or a detractor. The ideal scenario for a big brand is for buyers to keep buying it out of habit and not give their purchase any thought at all.

1.5 WHO IS RESPONSIBLE FOR BRANDING?

When companies are formed, the founders often have a clear reason for starting the business. This often defines what the brand stands for and shapes all the decision-making.

Accomplished rock climber Yvon Chouinard founded Chouinard Equipment (later Patagonia) in 1957. He had the ambition to produce sports equipment that would allow people to enjoy the great outdoors but have a minimal impact on the environment. How consumers saw the brand and what made it appealing stemmed from Yvon's vision and how he and his like-minded colleagues ran the business (see https://eu.patagonia.com/gb/en/company-history).

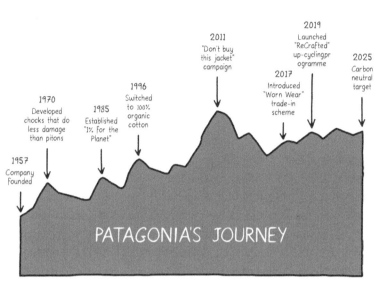

PATAGONIA'S JOURNEY

1957
Company
founded

1970
Developed
chocks that do
less damage
than pitons

1985
Established
"1% for the
Planet"

1996
Switched
to 100%
organic
cotton

2011
"Don't buy
this jacket"
campaign

2017
Introduced
"Worn Wear"
trade-in
scheme

2019
Launched
"ReCrafted"
up-cyclingpr
ogramme

2025
Carbon
neutral
target

Company founders often provide this clarity on branding. They may also inspire the whole company to operate in a way that projects the brand to the wider world. Companies with a leader who is passionate about the business are more likely to thrive. Apple lost its way in 1985 when its inspirational leader, Steve Jobs, left the business. It only found its mojo again when he returned in 1997. Many of today's biggest companies, including Amazon and Facebook, are still led by their founding entrepreneur.

How can organizations whose founders have departed maintain the same branding clarity of the early days? In these situations, marketers need to take the lead. Jim Stengel was Global Marketing Officer for Procter & Gamble between 2001 and 2008. He was the driving force behind the company's success over this period, during which its sales revenue doubled. Great marketers are futurists.

They can imagine how the company could address people's frustrations, needs and desires – and use this understanding to build the business. It's the chief marketing officer, rather than other board members, who can say, "This is what the world needs, and here's how we will deliver it."

One of the world's most successful companies over the past 50 years has been Nintendo. Having made playing cards and toys since 1889, the company expanded into video games in 1972. Since then, it has had four competent presidents, but they have all given the limelight to the company's talisman, Shigeru Miyamoto. 'Miyamoto-san' announces the company's most exciting new products with infectious, child-like enthusiasm. He is the company's chief marketing officer in all but name – his recent job titles include head of studio, representative director and creative fellow. His vision for new types of games and consoles has enabled Nintendo to broaden its user base.

Other organizations should look at Nintendo's example. People who understand consumer priorities should have control over innovation strategy and corporate direction, as well as marketing.

Of course, even the most gifted marketer cannot influence a company's fortunes unless they have the backing of the whole organization. For a marketing strategy to work, employees need to be aware of it, understand it, believe it and act upon it. One way of achieving this is to think like a boxer. Boxers need to understand their competitors' strengths and weaknesses, decide whom to challenge and in what order, make sure all parts of their body work together, build the necessary muscles and skills, and know how to always stay grounded. Marketers can use a similar checklist.

ENSURE YOUR STRATEGY PACKS A PUNCH

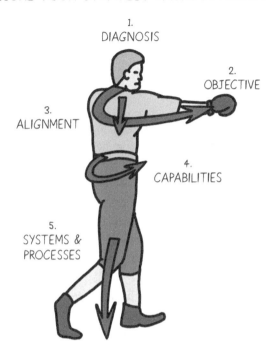

DIAGNOSIS

- What trends will affect our category and brand?
- How are consumer priorities changing?
- How is the competitive landscape evolving?
- What are our opportunities and barriers to growth?

OBJECTIVE

- What are our commercial goals? In one year? In five years?
- How does our brand need to evolve?

ALIGNMENT
- Does the whole organization understand and believe in the strategy?
- Does every team understand its role in delivering that strategy?

CAPABILITIES
- Are all corporate functions equipped to fulfil their role?
- What resources and skills do we need to develop?

SYSTEMS AND PROCESSES
- Do we have the systems and processes to ground the strategy in day-to-day business operations?
- Will we be able to track our progress? And provide early warnings so the business can course-correct?

Once your organization is fully prepared and match fit, your brand should be ready to take on all comers. Even then, you'll need the flexibility to think on your feet and adjust the strategy if circumstances change.

1.6 THE VALUE OF BRANDING

A brand with strong mental connections and responses can charge a higher price for the same volume as a competitor. That higher price can be cashed in to deliver an improved margin for the business or reinvested in the brand for future success. Investments might include more money being spent on innovation or brand-building advertising.

Alternatively, a strong brand can achieve a greater volume of sales at the same price. This makes it more attractive to distribution channels and creates efficiencies of scale in operations (sourcing raw materials, production, shipping, etc.).

In other words, strong branding shifts the demand curve for the brand. Most brands sell less if they raise their price. However, marketing that builds the brand enables it to charge more, or sell more at the existing price, and so generate more profit.

IMPACT OF BRAND-BUILDING ON DEMAND CURVE

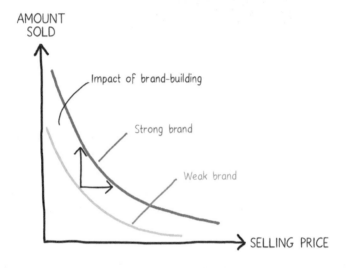

Branding (see *Section 1.2* for a definition) can be considered a good investment if it generates more profit than the cost of the activity.

Marketers face a challenge when making the case for brand-building investments. The financial upside often takes a long time to accrue. Take a new brand, for example. Early on, branding investment typically shows only a small return – less than the cost of the activity. The big payback occurs once the brand has become a serious contender with more established brands. It can take years of sustained activity to achieve this.

WHY BRAND BUILDING TAKES TIME TO WORK

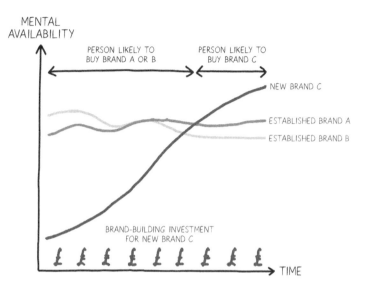

MENTAL AVAILABILITY

PERSON LIKELY TO BUY BRAND A OR B

PERSON LIKELY TO BUY BRAND C

NEW BRAND C

ESTABLISHED BRAND A

ESTABLISHED BRAND B

BRAND-BUILDING INVESTMENT FOR NEW BRAND C

TIME

When you factor in the long-term effects of brand-building, the return on investment can be high. As a rule of thumb, the long-term return on investment from advertising is more than double the return seen within the first 12 months on average (Binet and Field, 2013). It is often five or more times greater than the return seen within the first three months.

The Brand Value Growth Matrix shows how advertising amplifies the growth strong brands achieve. The matrix was developed by the author and Peter Walshe, former Global BRANDZ Director at Kantar Millward Brown. It compares the value of brands between 2006 and 2015.

BRAND VALUE GROWTH MATRIX

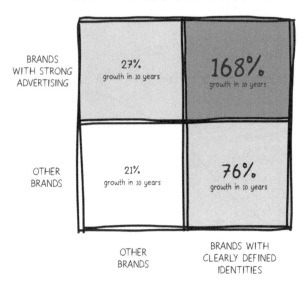

Brands with clearly defined identities, assessed by combining measures of distinctiveness and differentiation, grow more than other brands. However, brands with clear identities that promote themselves using strong advertising are the real winners. These brands grew by 168% over ten years. This compares to growth in the MSCI World Index of 71% over the same period. Strong brands deliver good returns; strong brands with great advertising deliver exceptional returns.

The commercial benefit of building a strong brand goes way beyond sales of the brand's initial product range. The success of the personal care brand Dove shows how success with a single product in one market can be a springboard for success across multiple product categories and geographies (see *Section 2.4* for more details).

Having a strong brand can also help a company attract the best talent and inspire employees to stay with the company and work productively. Marketing commentators often struggle to explain how Apple has developed such innovative products. One reason is that the world's best designers are keen to learn from the people they most admire. They want to work with people such as Steve Jobs and Jony Ive, so they apply for a job at Apple. The ability to attract and motivate high-calibre employees goes a long way to explain Apple's success. Apple produces great products thanks to its talented employees and how they work together. The best of the best work on high-priority developments and the environment allows them to create the optimum user experience.

APPLE INSPIRATION FOR PRODUCT LEADERSHIP

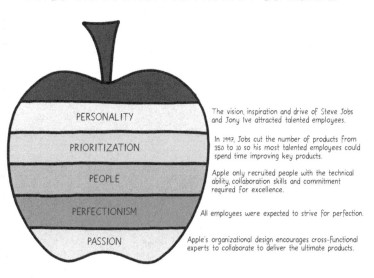

PERSONALITY — The vision, inspiration and drive of Steve Jobs and Jony Ive attracted talented employees.

PRIORITIZATION — In 1997, Jobs cut the number of products from 350 to 10 so his most talented employees could spend time improving key products.

PEOPLE — Apple only recruited people with the technical ability, collaboration skills and commitment required for excellence.

PERFECTIONISM — All employees were expected to strive for perfection.

PASSION — Apple's organizational design encourages cross-functional experts to collaborate to deliver the ultimate products.

CHAPTER 2

BRAND
DEVELOPMENT

2.1 NAMING YOUR BRAND

Names are important. Sales of the Patagonian toothfish saw a 30-fold increase in 90 days when it was rebadged Chilean sea bass in the late 1970s. Names shape how people perceive a brand and how easy it is for them to ask for it, search for it and recommend it to others. They also help people to distinguish products from alternatives and remember them. If a brand always delivers good quality, it will build a 'good name' for itself – an old phrase for an aspect of branding that will never become outdated.

When choosing a brand name, consider these five characteristics:

THE IDEAL BRAND NAME

NO NEGATIVE CONNOTATIONS

DISTINCTIVE

EASY TO SAY & SPELL

!?XX%!?}|

AVAILABLE

CATCHY

DISTINCTIVE

All brands should aim to be as distinctive as possible. Having a brand name that looks and sounds like no other is a major advantage. The Australian furniture polish Mr Sheen has a unique name that has become famous. A 'Mr Sheen' character features on its pack and in its advertising, alongside the slogan "Mr Sheen shines umpteen things clean." Together, these 'distinctive brand assets' (see *Chapter 3*) have helped make the brand highly salient and fuel its growth.

EASY TO SAY AND SPELL

If a brand name is easy to pronounce and spell, people can ask for it with ease, search for it and tell others about it. The handicap of having an awkward name can be overcome but it is better to avoid the problem in the first place. Realizing this issue, accounting software brand Xero used a voiceover in its advertising asking people to search for "Zero with an X." Czech beer brand Plzeňský Prazdroj became Pilsner Urquell in other countries to make pronunciation simpler in languages with a more inclusive attitude to vowels.

CATCHY

The article "The Sound of Brands" by researchers at the University of Alberta explains that names with a repetitive sound are more appealing, and this enhances brand preference and choice (Argo, Popa and Smith, 2010). Examples include Kit Kat, TikTok and Dunkin' Donuts.

AVAILABLE

An obvious consideration when choosing a brand name is whether it can be registered as a trademark in all potential markets. It is also relevant to check whether URLs related to the name are available.

NO NEGATIVE CONNOTATIONS

It makes sense to avoid names with negative associations. Poolife, for example, isn't an ideal name for a swimming pool maintenance company. International brands should also check what their name might sound like in different languages. Nova, for example, is a stellar name for a car in English-speaking countries, conjuring the concept of newness. In Spanish, however, it means 'not going.' Likewise, the name Smeg has connotations in English that are off-putting in a kitchen context.

Brand names can accumulate negative associations over time. For example, the name of the rice brand Uncle Ben's was changed to Ben's Original in 2020. Titles such as 'uncle' and 'aunt' had historically been used in southern US states to refer to black people, instead of the more formal and respectful 'mister' or 'miss.' Changing social attitudes meant that this was no longer deemed acceptable. At the same time, the stereotyped African American brand character was removed from the packaging.

It is unclear whether it is helpful for a name to convey what the brand is or does, or what differentiates it. Many brand names do give an impression of what the brand is all about. Facebook (formerly FaceMash) started as a website for students to rate fellow students' attractiveness. Convenience store Tote'm changed its name to 7-Eleven in 1946 to highlight its long opening hours. Groupon (group coupon), Netflix (internet flicks), TiVo (television input, video output) and Microsoft (microcomputer software) are all made-up words designed to convey a vague sense of what the brand does.

Likewise, little is known about the benefit of using existing words that bring with them positive connotations – for example, Dove (peace, freedom), Snuggle (comfort, affection) and EasyJet (convenience, speed). Given how the brain works, it is likely that brands can benefit from leveraging the meanings of existing words. However, names with no intrinsic meaning have also proven to be effective. Branding involves building associations around the brand to create saliency and meaning, so existing connotations aren't essential. This is why brands based on their founder's name can work well. Examples include Dyson, Rolls-Royce, Kellogg's and Heinz. DKNY comes from Donna Karan New York. IKEA came from the name of the founder, Ingvar Kamprad; Elmtaryd, the farm on which he grew up; and the nearby village of Agunnaryd.

2.2 BRAND ARCHITECTURE

Corporate growth often depends on a company building or buying multiple brands. These may exist within one or several product categories. Such a strategy can provide economies of scale. It also reduces risk. If one brand is struggling to grow, profits can be diverted to brands or categories with greater growth potential. Volkswagen Group, for example, owns many car brands. These include Škoda, SEAT, Volkswagen, Audi, Porsche, Lamborghini and Bentley. This allows Volkswagen to dominate the car industry. It uses different brands to appeal to consumers with different priorities and budgets. At the same time, it saves money by sharing new technologies across the group. It also uses sub-brands to cater for people at different life stages, looking for cars of different sizes (Up!, Golf, Passat, Sharan, etc.). By doing this, Volkswagen can tailor its messages and media choices for each sub-brand so that it reaches and influences each target audience.

Yet managing a portfolio of brands represents a major marketing challenge. An architect decides how to connect different spaces. Likewise, a brand manager must define the architecture that will benefit their company. Then they need to build it. The human mind makes connections based on what it experiences. Names, logos, packaging styles, and owned and paid media all influence brand connections. Marketers manage all these touchpoints to construct the desired brand architecture.

In 2000, David Aaker and Erich Joachimsthaler introduced the Brand Relationship Spectrum. It describes the various ways brands and sub-brands can be connected. Aaker and Joachimsthaler identified four approaches. Organizations use one approach or a mixture of approaches and tend to evolve their naming strategies over time.

BRAND RELATIONSHIP SPECTRUM

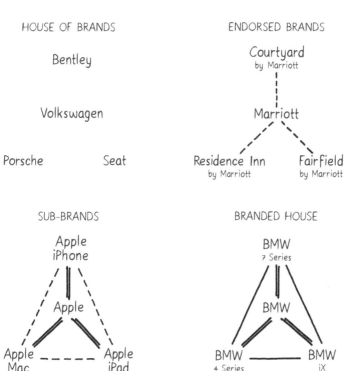

HOUSE OF BRANDS

A house of brands is a model in which the organization (or 'house') keeps its brands entirely separate. A few consumers and people working within the industry may be aware that the brands have the same owner, but the connection is largely irrelevant from a branding point of view. Volkswagen Group, for example, doesn't publicize that it owns luxury brands Bentley and Porsche as well as budget brands Škoda and Seat. Building an association between these brands would not be desirable. It could even be detrimental. After all, prestige and low price do not sit well together. Linking brands with their parent company can, however, be worthwhile on occasion. When Volkswagen acquired Škoda and improved its cars in 2000, it connected the brand with the Volkswagen name because that carried stronger perceptions of quality.

ENDORSED BRANDS

Endorsed brands are brands that have their own identity but are connected with a familiar, respected parent brand. The strength of the parent helps to make the endorsed brand more credible and appealing. A new fragrance called Obsession could easily be dismissed. Consumers are more likely to pay attention to a new brand called Obsession by Calvin Klein.

This 'halo effect' (see *page 39*) can work the other way around too. Unilever has often devoted a second or two at the end of its brands' TV ads to mentioning the corporation's name. The idea is to make potential investors aware of all the famous household brands Unilever owns. The approach also lends credibility to new Unilever brands when they launch.

SUB-BRANDS

Many brands adopt a sub-brand strategy. This is like the endorsed brands approach, but the sub-brands' names include the master brand. This strengthens the link between master and sub-brand. It also strengthens the connection between the sub-brands. A positive experience with one sub-brand generates interest in affiliated sub-brands. Apple has created an ecosystem that enhances the user experience if people buy into the whole range. This strategy also allows sub-brands to develop associations uniquely relevant to their areas, while benefiting from the broader associations of the master brand.

The relative levels of importance of the master brand and the sub-brand vary and can change over time. For example, Sony PlayStation's early success was boosted by the familiarity and reputation of the Sony name. Over time, the PlayStation name has become more salient and respected in its own right.

BRANDED HOUSE

In a branded house, the master brand name is all-important. The brand's different product ranges have their own signifiers, but they are not intended to have different identities. All products share the properties and values of the master brand. The branded house approach is the purest approach from a branding point of view. Advertising for the master brand has a positive effect on the whole product range. Advertising for an individual brand also affects the sales of others. This is known as an advertising 'halo effect.'

Unilever pioneered the use of halos in the 1990s with its personal care brand Dove. It found that the effects were strongest between product areas with a lot in common. For example, sales of Dove's cleansing bar increased when Dove's shampoo was advertised. The benefit was greatest when consistent aesthetics and communication themes were used. Dove uses master brand advertising to build memorability and emotional affinity. Alongside this, the brand advertises specific ranges. The range advertising focuses principally on product benefits. All Dove products have skincare properties; this is always part of the communication.

Aaker and Joachimsthaler suggest that the branded house should be the default architecture. Alternatives should be considered by answering these four questions:

- Does the master brand contribute to the offering?
- Will the master brand be strengthened by association with the new offering?
- Is there a compelling need for a separate brand?
- Will the business support a new brand name?

Companies that manage multiple brands may adopt a combination of the approaches described above. Apple, for example, uses the house of brands approach for Beats and Mobeewave; the endorsed brands approach for iPhone, iPad, iPod and iMac; and the branded house model for Apple Watch, Apple Music (formerly Apple iTunes) and Apple TV.

Brand managers need to think about where synergies exist to determine where and how to connect their portfolio. Once a clear brand architecture exists, it should be used to guide naming decisions, media strategy and messaging.

2.3 DEFINING YOUR BRAND

Brand growth requires a clear vision of a brand that people will love and marketing activation that brings the vision to life.

You can define what you want your brand to become using the Brand PIÑATA, first introduced in *The Smart Marketing Book* (White, 2020). Here's an example of the PIÑATA applied to the Snickers snack food brand.

BRAND PIÑATA SNICKERS EXAMPLE

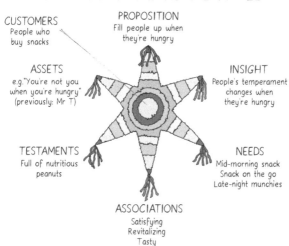

CUSTOMERS
People who buy snacks

PROPOSITION
Fill people up when they're hungry

ASSETS
e.g."You're not you when you're hungry" (previously: Mr T)

INSIGHT
People's temperament changes when they're hungry

TESTAMENTS
Full of nutritious peanuts

NEEDS
Mid-morning snack
Snack on the go
Late-night munchies

ASSOCIATIONS
Satisfying
Revitalizing
Tasty

Defining your brand in this way enables you to manage your marketing mix. Product, price, place and promotion all contribute to how people see your brand. A PIÑATA is a business's guide to ensure all activities convey a clear, coherent idea of the brand.

The vision may exist, fully formed, at the beginning of the brand's life. Often, this comes from the founder's reason for bringing the brand to market. More often, the brand definition evolves as the team managing it learns from experience what resonates with consumers, or the brand is forced to change because of shifts in the competitive landscape or consumer priorities.

Market research can play a vital role in developing or evolving the definition. Brand owners used to conduct studies to identify the needs and priorities of different groups of category buyers. Then they'd pick segment(s) to target and then focus their efforts on these types of people, particularly when advertising the brand. The flaw in this approach has been highlighted by Byron Sharp from the Ehrenberg-Bass Institute. Focusing on a subset of category buyers limits a brand's growth potential. People enter and leave the category all the time and their needs are constantly shifting. Focusing on a small subset of current category buyers means your brand remains unknown to other people who will soon be ripe to buy your brand.

A better approach is to aim for your brand to come to mind across a range of different usage contexts (which Sharp refers to as "category entry points"). If you do this, whenever someone has a certain need-state, they are likely to buy your brand. Sharp describes this as building "mental market share" in his influential book *How Brands Grow* (2010).

MENTAL MARKET SHARE

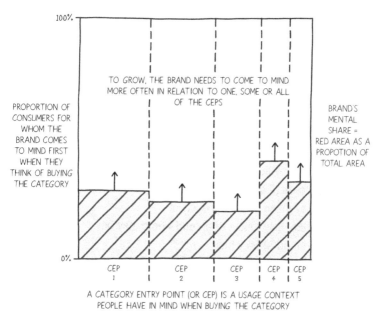

A CATEGORY ENTRY POINT (OR CEP) IS A USAGE CONTEXT
PEOPLE HAVE IN MIND WHEN BUYING THE CATEGORY

There remains a debate, however, about whether a brand should aim to become all things to everyone. The author's point of view is that a brand should focus on a small number of usage contexts and dominate these before expanding to others. Also, a brand should not attempt to become a 'jack of all trades.' Given how the mind works, it is difficult for a brand to come to mind for different usage contexts that have conflicting mental connections. For example, it's hard to imagine how a brand with a rich set of mental associations suggesting 'cheap and cheerful' (e.g. George by ASDA) could evolve so that it would come to mind when people were looking for opulent luxury (e.g. Gucci).

With this in mind, the focus of market research needs to move away from consumer segments and towards usage contexts. The author recommends a three-stage approach to obtain the required insights.

1 ESTABLISH BUYING ATTITUDES AND PROFILES

This is done via a survey of a representative sample of category buyers, who are asked for detail about themselves and their relationship with the category:

- Why they buy the category
- The process (if any) they use to decide which brands to consider
- How they make their final decision
- How often, how much, when and where they buy
- Which brand(s) they buy
- Their mental associations with different brands and their responses to these
- Their demographic, psychographic and lifestyle characteristics

In some countries and categories, this data will already exist. A panel provider such as Kantar Worldpanel (https://www.kantar.com/expertise/consumer-shopper-retail/consumer-panels) may be able to provide the data and analyse it for you. If not, you will need to do your own study. You may also need to conduct qualitative research before the survey to reveal all the relevant parameters and ensure the questionnaire reflects how different people think and behave.

2 QUANTIFY USAGE CONTEXTS

The data from the previous stage is combined to identify a set of usage contexts that between them represent most of the category purchases. For most categories, the top eight to 12 usage contexts should be enough. Here's an example of what some of the main usage contexts might be for a snack category:

- Mid-morning snack
- For when I'm on the go
- To give as a gift
- For grazing during the day
- To treat myself
- A healthy way to keep me going
- Evening snack
- Instead of a meal
- For sharing with friends

It is vital for marketeers to know the relative sizes of these usage contexts. This information indicates which areas would offer the greatest growth potential should the brand be able to dominate them. Also, the nature of the usage contexts suggests the kinds of innovation and communications that would be most relevant.

3 CHOOSE USAGE CONTEXT(S) TO TARGET

The choice involves complex considerations. It requires the combination of data, company and competitor knowledge, branding expertise and creative thinking:

- Would the usage context(s) be large enough to support your growth ambitions?
- Do any other brands already dominate the usage context(s)?
- Could your brand satisfy the usage context better than competitors?

- Would the required repositioning be credible for your brand?
- What impact would choosing these usage contexts have on your other brands?

Knowing which usage contexts you are going to target in the short and long term goes a long way towards completing your brand PIÑATA and setting yourself up for success. To achieve sustained success, your company needs to be able to deliver well against your chosen usage contexts. Aldi is one of the world's fastest-growing supermarket brands. It aims to sell products of at least comparable quality to its competitors at a lower price. It can do this and still make a good profit because all aspects of its operations are designed to keep costs down.

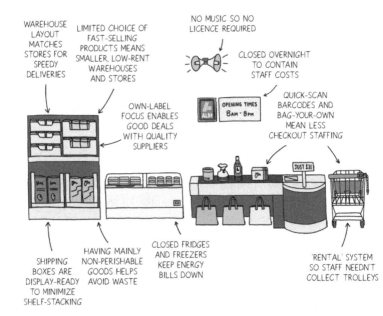

WAREHOUSE LAYOUT MATCHES STORES FOR SPEEDY DELIVERIES

LIMITED CHOICE OF FAST-SELLING PRODUCTS MEANS SMALLER, LOW-RENT WAREHOUSES AND STORES

NO MUSIC SO NO LICENCE REQUIRED

CLOSED OVERNIGHT TO CONTAIN STAFF COSTS

OWN-LABEL FOCUS ENABLES GOOD DEALS WITH QUALITY SUPPLIERS

OPENING TIMES 8AM - 8PM

QUICK-SCAN BARCODES AND BAG-YOUR-OWN MEAN LESS CHECKOUT STAFFING

JUST £1!

SHIPPING BOXES ARE DISPLAY-READY TO MINIMIZE SHELF-STACKING

HAVING MAINLY NON-PERISHABLE GOODS HELPS AVOID WASTE

CLOSED FRIDGES AND FREEZERS KEEP ENERGY BILLS DOWN

'RENTAL' SYSTEM SO STAFF NEEDN'T COLLECT TROLLEYS

Even a well-established brand can grow by creating a strong connection with a major usage context. In the early 2000s, UK supermarket chain Sainsbury's was struggling. Sales had been in decline for years. In 2004, new CEO Justin King set an ambitious £2.5 billion sales target over three years. This inspired the brand's "Try something new today" campaign, featuring celebrity chef Jamie Oliver.

Try something new today

The advertising provided homemakers with ideas for tasty, everyday family meals, while highlighting the few extra ingredients they'd need to buy. It worked brilliantly. The campaign attracted new customers and boosted the value of shoppers' weekly bill. Sales increased across the whole product range, not just the featured ingredients. The campaign's success came from associating Sainsbury's with a frequently recurring challenge common to many shoppers – providing a variety of family-friendly meals day in, day out.

2.4 PLANNING FOR EXPANSION

The growth of any brand will plateau if it is successful with its initial product range in its region of origin. Further growth must come from expanding the product range, extending geographically or both. Before scaling your brand, the business fundamentals need to be in place. Investors seem keen to fund technology-based brands even if they have never made a profit, but this isn't wise. According to Cyrine Ben-Hafaïedh and Anaïs Hamelin (2022), profit-focused brands are better set for future growth. By contrast, unprofitable, growth-focused brands have a comparatively smaller chance of making a long-term profit.

As brands grow, they may enjoy efficiencies of scale or be able to leverage their growing consumer base. However, these benefits often reflect wishful thinking rather than sound business analysis.

THE PATH TO PROFITABLE GROWTH

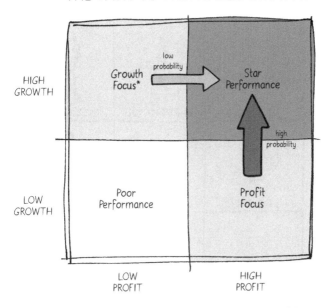

*Growth-focused brands are also much more likely to fall into poor performance over time than profit-focused brands

If your brand is profitable, the Enhanced Ansoff Matrix (Johannesson, 2009) illustrates the complex choices you'll need to make when considering your next step for driving growth. The matrix highlights nine possible growth strategies. You could continue selling your existing product(s), introduce enhanced or modified version(s), or develop completely new products. You could also decide to focus on your current audience, expand to new markets or target different types of consumer.

ENHANCED ANSOFF MATRIX

	EXISTING PRODUCT	MODIFIED PRODUCT	NEW PRODUCTS
NEW TARGET GROUPS	MARKET DEVELOPMENT	PARTIAL DIVERSIFICATION	DIVERSIFICATION
NEW MARKETS	MARKET EXPANSION	LIMITED DIVERSIFICATION	PARTIAL DIVERSIFICATION
EXISTING MARKET/ TARGET GROUP	MARKET PENETRATION	PRODUCT MODIFICATION	PRODUCT DEVELOPMENT

The personal care brand Dove was launched in 1957. During its early years, the brand focused on building penetration of its cleansing bar in a few key markets, targeting women (market penetration). The advertising explained that Dove's cleansing bar contained moisturizer and was pH neutral, so it cared for the skin (unlike traditional soap). Over the next 38 years, Dove launched its cleansing bar in new markets across the world (market expansion). It wasn't until 1995 that Dove started to launch products in other product areas, still targeting women (product development). This started with adjacent categories, such as shower gel and shampoo.

In 2010, Dove launched Dove Men + Care. In 2017, it introduced Baby Dove. These new ranges mainly comprised modified versions of existing Dove products (partial diversification).

As of 2022, Dove sells more than 150 products and operates in more the 150 countries across the world. The brand has been successful because:
- It has built strong associations with skincare over time
- It launched new products and targeted new consumer types after establishing high levels of familiarity and trust
- Its products are consistently high quality and deliver against the brand's skincare promise

Deciding which strategy is right for your brand is complicated. Whether to expand to new markets, for example, depends on the size of the opportunity compared to the investment required. The costs of transportation, retail distribution, advertising and legal matters all need to be considered. You may need to produce modified versions of your product to succeed in new contexts. Even Coca-Cola varies its formula to reflect regional taste preferences.

Growth planning also requires an understanding of how consumers' needs and priorities are likely to evolve. Google Trends allows brand managers to identify trends that will have an impact on category growth and the fortunes of their brand. For example, the cleaning product manufacturer Method identified an opportunity for a brand that is less harmful to the environment and looks great in the kitchen, based on consumer feedback.

METHOD UNIQUENESS EXAMPLE

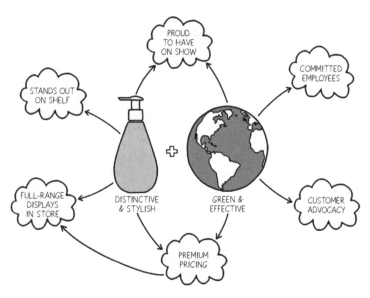

The company reinforces its commitment to environmental care through its eco-friendly factories and ongoing "People against dirty" campaign. Method promotes the idea of removing dirt without dirtying the environment. The appeal of its products is amplified by their elegant packaging. The combination of eco-friendliness and unique product design has fuelled the brand's phenomenal success. Since its launch in 2001, Method has grown to be worth more than $130 million (2021), despite competing with the three most sophisticated packaged goods companies in the world. The founders attribute this success to their strong company culture, which prizes originality, the total alignment of staff behind what the brand stands for, and having a brand that is highly distinctive and differentiated from the competition (see https://www.youtube.com/watch?v=IMSNgmAC_BQ).

2.5 PURPOSE-LED BRANDING

From an ethical point of view, brands should operate in a way that respects the earth's limited resources and fragile ecosystem. Whether a brand should leverage its commitment to a societal cause or benefit in order to gain a competitive advantage is a different matter.

The various ways in which a brand might reflect such a commitment can be shown in a Venn diagram. If the commitment amounts to no more than the company taking steps to become more socially or environmentally responsible, then advertising these steps is unlikely to have a significant brand-building effect – after all, lots of other companies are doing similar things. There is, however, a brand-building opportunity from building a strong association between the brand and a particular social issue (or set of related issues) by making it a major theme of the brand's communication over an extended period. This approach is likely to backfire, however, if the company's actions are found to be inconsistent with the stance taken by its brand(s). For example, Unilever had to rethink its advertising for the male grooming brand Lynx/Axe because the way it portrayed women was seen by some as being contradictory to the values of another Unilever brand, Dove.

BRAND PURPOSE VENN DIAGRAM

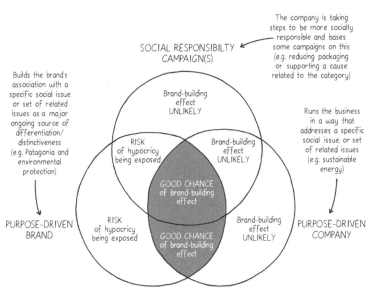

In the long run, only brands that practise what they preach will be able to leverage their connection with the cause they support.

Empirical evidence suggests that 'brand purpose' campaigns are no more effective than any other type of communication, as Peter Field (2021) argues. He identified 47 'purpose' campaigns from the databank held by the UK'S Institute of Advertising Practitioners – i.e. campaigns with objectives related to an environmental or societal cause beyond what the brand is/does. Field compared their effectiveness with the other 333 campaigns in the databank from the same time period.

EFFECTIVENESS OF BRAND PURPOSE CAMPAIGNS

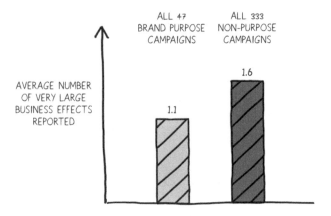

However, these findings do not tell the full story, as Field has pointed out. Some of the brand purpose campaigns included in the analysis were highly effective. Further, the brands varied in terms of their long-term commitment to the cause they featured in their advertising. For some brands, the cause dictates business operations and is the basis of most brand communications. For other brands, brand purpose amounts to no more than publicizing small changes to business operations with a societal benefit.

Outdoor clothing and equipment brand Patagonia sits at the centre of the Venn diagram (see *Section 1.5* for more details). In the author's opinion, brands should communicate about societal or environmental issues if the organization is genuinely committed to the cause and it is relevant to the brand's identity. Commitment to a cause is a company decision, not a communications option. Marketers should only consider communication about a cause if the brand or company sits in positions 1 or 2 in the Venn diagram above.

2.6 GLOBAL BRANDING

For a brand to succeed internationally, it usually needs to tailor its product and communications to local markets. If you browse the top ten programmes on Netflix by country (top10.netflix.com), you'll see little overlap between the most popular content in the US and India, for example. Netflix excels at providing high-quality content and a great user experience, but the content it promotes varies by market.

A brand's global growth opportunity depends on whether people in different countries have similar needs, priorities and preferences related to the category. What, when and with whom people eat varies hugely by culture – whereas people's use of mobile phones is relatively similar the world over. This explains why the food and drink brand Knorr has different ranges of products in different regions. Samsung, however, can launch the same models across many markets and use similar advertising.

Brands that succeed globally tend to have an offer that is universally relevant. Take Red Bull, for example. People all over the world have the need for an energy boost from time to time. Red Bull originated in Thailand as Krating Daeng (literally 'the Red Bull'). It contains caffeine to keep you alert and taurine to make you calm and focused. The original drink was popular among labourers looking for ways to help them get through the working day. Austrian entrepreneur Dietrich Mateschitz discovered the brand when it helped him recover from jetlag on a trip to Asia. He added the fizz and launched the drink across Europe at a premium price. The brand gained distribution through positioning as the first in a sector that was new to Europe – energy drinks. In the UK, the brand achieved early sales not from labourers but from party animals. Clubbers started using Red Bull to keep their energy levels up all night by using it as a mixer.

Alongside its product benefits, Red Bull's long-term growth has been attributed to the strength of its promotional activity and advertising. The company has done a phenomenal job of building a strong brand. *In How Brands Grow* (2010), Byron Sharp introduced the concept of "mental availability" – the probability that a buyer will notice, recognize and/or think of a brand in buying situations (see *Section 1.3*). Red Bull is an example of a brand that has built high mental availability by using a consistent set of distinctive assets (see *Chapter 3*) in all its communications since launch. By sponsoring Formula 1 and other extreme sports both globally and locally, Red Bull has created a vibrant and compelling brand in consumers' minds. Launched in 1987, the brand reached sales of more than 8 billion cans per year worldwide by 2020.

RED BULL EXAMPLE

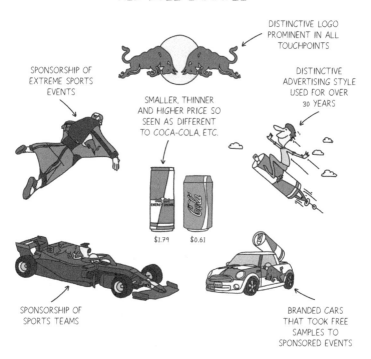

DISTINCTIVE LOGO PROMINENT IN ALL TOUCHPOINTS

SPONSORSHIP OF EXTREME SPORTS EVENTS

DISTINCTIVE ADVERTISING STYLE USED FOR OVER 30 YEARS

SMALLER, THINNER AND HIGHER PRICE SO SEEN AS DIFFERENT TO COCA-COLA, ETC.

$1.79 $0.61

SPONSORSHIP OF SPORTS TEAMS

BRANDED CARS THAT TOOK FREE SAMPLES TO SPONSORED EVENTS

Some brands take a lot longer before they thrive in overseas markets. The chocolate snack KitKat, created by the UK company Rowntree's and now produced by Nestlé, was launched in Japan in 1973 but only took off in the mid-2000s. By 2014, it had become the country's top-selling confection. Success came from leveraging two cultural phenomena.

Omiyage is the tradition of travellers bringing home local delicacies as gifts. KitKat saw an opportunity to draw on this custom, and create interest in a category devoid of innovation, by producing flavour variants inspired by the cuisines of Japan's different regions. In 2000, a strawberry KitKat was launched exclusively in Hokkaido, a popular holiday destination. It was a big hit. Since then, there have been more than 300 variants – mainly regional, seasonal or limited editions. The desire to try these variants, like collecting rare Pokémon, is amplified by the 'scarcity bias.' (see https://en.wikipedia.org/wiki/Scarcity_(social_psychology).

KITKAT JAPAN LOCALIZATION EXAMPLE

Omamori are lucky charms sold at Shinto shrines and Buddhist temples. 'KitKat' is pronounced 'kitto katto' in Japanese, which as it happens sounds like *kitto kastsu*, a phrase meaning 'you will surely win.' Nestlé found that KitKat sales spiked every January because parents gave the snack to their children before their exams to wish them good luck. This inspired Nestlé to promote the brand as a token of good fortune (see *Section 6.5*). Nestlé's success in Japan has encouraged greater innovation within the KitKat brand in other markets.

Nappy brand Pampers shows how a brand can have a consistent global positioning but tailor its messaging to local markets.

THE PAMPERS BRAND

Pampers had become a market leader in many Western markets by focusing on the product's superior dryness and comfort. In the West, parents see these as priorities for keeping their baby happy and healthy. In China, however, this messaging is less effective. Following a couple of false starts, Pampers took off in China in 2007, nine years after launch. Market research revealed that the quality of a baby's sleep, and its impact on child development, is more important to Chinese parents. This inspired the highly effective "Golden Sleep" advertising. The campaign highlighted clinical research proving that Pampers enables babies to get a better night's sleep. It featured a photomontage of babies sleeping that broke records in terms of the number of photos included. According to David Aaker (2013), the campaign resulted in a 55% sales increase.

CHAPTER 3

DISTINCTIVE
BRAND ASSETS

3.1 WHAT ARE DISTINCTIVE BRAND ASSETS?

Distinctive brand assets are any images, shapes, colours, sounds, words, rituals or characters that come to mind when people think about or come across a brand. The most effective assets don't come to mind in association with competitor brands.

Distinctive assets are hugely important to brands. They help to make brands more salient and advertising more effective. It is hard to think of any successful brand that has not leveraged the value of distinctive brand assets.

WHY DISTINCTIVE BRAND ASSETS ARE VALUABLE

ANCHORING BRAND
MEMORIES

EVOKING BRAND
AT POINT OF SALE

MAKING COMMUNICATIONS
MORE EFFICIENT

GENERATING
APPEAL

ANCHORING BRAND MEMORIES

Distinctive assets help to anchor all the memories related to a brand in people's minds. When people encounter an asset, other memories related to the brand are brought to mind. This helps the brand feel familiar and relevant, and also increases the chance it will be chosen.

EVOKING BRAND AT POINT OF SALE

Brand assets play a vital role if people are exposed to them close to the moment of purchase. Doing this brings the brand (and its associations) to mind at the perfect time. A character on the packaging of a retail product, for example, can evoke brand memories just as people decide which brand to buy. A slogan appearing in a sponsored search result can remind people of what a brand stands for and encourage them to click on the link.

People often don't have the time or inclination to give much thought to what they buy, especially in everyday, low-cost categories. Any brand that is salient at the crucial moment has a great chance of being chosen. If someone often buys your brand, exposing them to brand assets can help to seal the deal and prevent other brands from being considered.

MAKING COMMUNICATIONS MORE EFFICIENT

Brands with established assets can use them to make their communications more effective. Featuring assets in an ad brings the brand to the forefront of people's minds as they experience the ad. This makes it easier for everything else in the ad to become connected with and remembered in association with the brand. This works because of how memories are created. Any two things that are simultaneously present in human attention get linked together.

Ivan Pavlov proved this when his dogs started salivating whenever they heard a bell ringing, provided the sound had been repeatedly associated at mealtimes.

GENERATING APPEAL

Some assets may also contribute to the affinity people feel towards a brand. The fabric conditioner brand Snuggle, for example, has used a puppet teddy bear as its mascot since 1986. The bear, created by Kermit Love from Jim Henson's Creature Shop, makes people think of softness and caring. These concepts are known to be motivating when people are buying a fabric conditioner.

Given the benefits distinctive brand assets can bring, every brand should aim to build several of them over time. There is no magic number but brands that manage their assets well tend to have five or six of them, in the author's experience. You might consider the following:

- A highly distinctive logo
- A colour scheme of no more than three colours
  (e.g. McDonald's use yellow, red and green)
- A visual asset (e.g. the 'golden arches')
- A sonic device and/or piece of music for all your audio and audio-visual touchpoints (e.g. "Ba da ba ba ba")
- A slogan (e.g. "I'm Lovin' It")
- A character or celebrity (e.g. Ronald McDonald)
- A shape-based asset related to your product or packaging
  (e.g. the unique cardboard containers McDonald's uses to serve fries)
- A brand ritual (see *Section 3.2*)

3.2 DISTINCTIVE BRAND ASSET EXAMPLES

DISTINCTIVE BRAND ASSETS DEFINITION

IMAGES

CHARACTERS/ CELEBRITIES

COLOURS

SHAPES

RITUALS

TYPEFACES

WORDS

JUST DO IT.

SOUNDS/ MUSIC

"Holidays are coming..."

SHAPES

Having a uniquely shaped pack or product is an effective way to make a brand distinctive. Toblerone, Volkswagen Beetle and Dyson are examples. Even though Coca-Cola sells few of its famous glass bottles, it still tends to use them in its advertising. Brand logos are where colour and shape are used together to help create a unique identity for a brand.

COLOURS

In the UK, if you show someone a shiny purple colour and ask them what brand it makes them think of, the majority will say Cadbury. Vodafone uses the same red colour in all its stores and advertising. 'Owning' a colour in this way is extremely valuable. It means that any promotional content featuring the colour (or shape – see below) will immediately bring the brand name to mind, provided the category is also cued in people's minds. If the memories triggered by the asset are positive, the brand is even more likely to be purchased.

IMAGES

Most people agree that sight is our primary sense. We store images in our memory to help us recall experiences that resonated with us and remember their meaning. People can still recall the imagery from early Apple iPod advertising. It showed dancing figures with earphones in silhouette, set against a brightly coloured background. Brand teams should decide the types of imagery, and even specific images, that they want to become associated with their brand.

CHARACTERS OR CELEBRITIES

Many successful brands have featured characters in their advertising and on their packaging for years or even decades. Examples include the Jolly Green Giant, Tony the Tiger (Kellogg's Frosties), the Michelin Man, Flat Eric (Levi's), Pillsbury Doughboy, Ronald McDonald, the M&Ms characters, Chester Cheetah (Cheetos), meerkats (Comparethemarket.com), the Energizer/Duracell Bunny, Colonel Sanders (Kentucky Fried Chicken) and of course Mickey Mouse (Disney). Historical and invented characters are ideal because brands can use them however they wish.

Associating your brand with a current celebrity, on the other hand, has both upsides and downsides. The upside is that people are hugely influenced by celebrities they know and love, even if they are endorsing a brand they have no qualifications to talk about. George Clooney is a sophisticated man, right? He must know good coffee when he tastes it, so Nespresso must be top-notch.

The downside is that celebrities are unpredictable and expensive, and have limited time to make ads. Soon after Yardley chose Helena Bonham Carter as their spokesperson, she told the press, "I don't know why Yardley chose me. I don't wear much make-up" (Caesar, 2005). Celebrities are a sure-fire way of generating attention for your brand. They are worth the money if they endorse the brand on and off screen, and if they are used for long enough to become a genuine brand asset.

RITUALS

Associating a ritual with your brand can help it become more memorable, associate it with specific usage occasions and heighten people's regard for it. Brand rituals are effective because:

- They activate multiple memory mechanisms – for example, sight and sound when someone bangs a Terry's Chocolate Orange on a table. This helps the brand to be memorable and come to mind again in similar contexts.

- They heighten anticipation of using the product, which means people's reward sensation lasts longer. Unboxing an Apple product, for example, is a pleasure in its own right.

- They can create an expectation of a good experience. For example, watching a bartender artfully pulling a perfect Guinness may enhance people's appreciation of the drink.

- If shared with others, the ritual connects the brand with the social world – for example, twisting, licking and dunking Oreos with the family. The Orangina ritual is to "shake the bottle, wake the drink". Rituals like this make the brand distinctive and connect the brand with feelings of sociability and security.

RITUALS INVENTED TO MAKE
BRANDS DISTINCTIVE

SOUNDS OR MUSIC

Brands can also leverage sounds to create strong, distinctive memories. The author can't help but sing "Did somebody say Just Eat?" (not always in his head) at the sight of a Just Eat logo. The few seconds this takes are enough to bring to mind everything the brand stands for and perhaps even a gentle smile. In the 1990s, the microprocessor brand Intel struggled to find a way to visualize what set it apart from its competitors. Instead, the brand used a sonic device in all its advertising to build a distinct identity in people's minds. McDonald's has used its "ba da ba ba ba" sound since 2003. Music can make a powerful brand asset. British department store John Lewis and Partners has leveraged the emotional power of well-known music in its much-anticipated Christmas ads since 2009.

WORDS

Like jingles, slogans (or 'taglines') can be effective for brand-building. "Just Do It" is as important to Nike as its 'swoosh'. Both help to make the brand distinctive and have the bonus of triggering feelings of empowerment and optimism. A catchy slogan that helps people remember your brand and what it stands for is worth its weight in gold. Here are some of the author's all-time favourites:

- BMW: "The ultimate driving machine."
- L'Oréal: "Because you're worth it."
- Kellogg's Rice Krispies: "Snap! Crackle! Pop!"
- Kentucky Fried Chicken: "Finger lickin' good."
- American Express: "Don't live life without it."
- Audi: "Vorsprung durch Technik."
- Maybelline: "Maybe she's born with it. Maybe it's Maybelline."
- Nintendo Pokémon: "Gotta catch 'em all."
- Mastercard: "There are some things money can't buy. For everything else, there's MasterCard."
- Dollar Shave Club: "Shave time. Shave money."

TYPEFACES

Anything used consistently has the potential to grow into a brand asset – even the shape of the lettering used in the logo and the brand's communications. Unusual, bespoke typefaces work best. Close your eyes and see whether you can visualize the typefaces used by these brands: Disney, SEGA, Yves Saint Laurent, H&M and Hershey's.

3.3 CHOOSING YOUR ASSETS

Jenni Romaniuk, author of *Building Distinctive Brand Assets* (2018), is a leading authority on this topic. Romaniuk advises that brands should focus on identifying or creating assets that are unique, and then investing in them so they become famous for the brand.

DISTINCTIVE ASSETS GRID

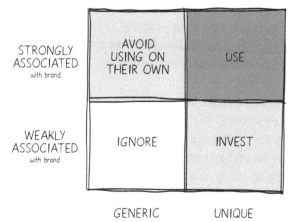

	GENERIC	UNIQUE
STRONGLY ASSOCIATED with brand	AVOID USING ON THEIR OWN	USE
WEAKLY ASSOCIATED with brand	IGNORE	INVEST

When developing a new brand, marketers should dedicate time to considering the assets they want to become associated with the brand. The more distinctive the asset, the better. Marketers need to ask:

- Is this asset useful in lots of contexts (pack, product, advertising, point of sale, etc.)?
- Could any other brand be associated with it?
- Has something like this already been used that could cause confusion?
- Will I be able to invest enough to own a category-generic asset, or do I need to use something novel?

Established brands should review their assets, identifying which to continue using and which new ones to introduce. If the brand has strong visual assets, it might be worth introducing an audio asset, for example. Since its formation in 1974, British Airways has been associated with the Union Jack Flag. In 1984, the brand introduced an audio element to its branding – "The Flower Duet" by Léo Delibes from the opera *Lakmé*. At the time of writing, it still uses this in its advertising, lounges and planes.

Singapore Airlines pioneered the use of aroma to create a distinctive brand experience. In 1990, it introduced a scent called Stefan Floridian Waters. It was infused into the airline's hot towels, sprayed into the cabins and even worn by cabin crew as their perfume. Leveraging an aroma as a distinctive brand asset is effective because the sense of smell arouses primal instincts (Walsh, 2020). Smell also helps experiences to go into the long-term memory and be retrieved more easily.

Marketers often ask whether brand assets need to be meaningful in some way. The jury is still out on this question. It's clear that assets can be effective without being meaningful – so long as they are distinctive. Czech bank ČSOB, for example, has built a strong association with a chameleon. Arguably, an armadillo or pangolin might have conveyed more relevant associations for a bank since they might convey the idea of protection or security. Yet the chameleon has been hugely successful and popular with both employees and customers. The author would argue that it is a bonus if a brand's assets have connotations that are relevant to category decision-making.

3.4 BUILDING YOUR ASSETS

Distinctive assets form a link with a brand through repeated exposure. Repetition is required because this helps long-term memories to be formed. Marketers should therefore avoid chopping and changing a brand's visual identity or advertising style. The trick to connecting assets with a brand is simple – feature them across all possible touchpoints, as often as you can. The repetition makes the mental connection stronger.

The value of consistency over time is illustrated by many of the biggest brands on the planet:

- McDonald's has used the phrase "I'm loving it" and the associated tune in almost all its advertising since 2003
- The Intel 'bong' sonic logo was introduced in 1994 to launch the brand's Pentium processor and has been used ever since
- Nike has partnered with Michael Jordan since 1985
- L'Oréal has used the phrase "Because you're worth it" or a close variation since 1971
- Kentucky Fried Chicken has used the phrase "Finger lickin' good" since 1956
- PG Tips featured chimpanzees in its advertising between 1956 and 2001

- The Marlboro Man was featured in Marlboro cigarette advertising between 1954 and 1999
- Tony the Tiger first appeared in advertising for Kellogg's Frosties in 1951
- De Beers has used the slogan "A diamond is forever" since 1947
- The Michelin Man first appeared at the World Fair in Lyon in 1894

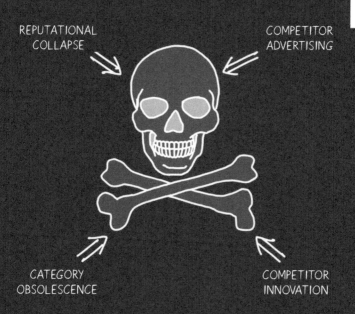

CHAPTER 4

REPUTATIONAL
COLLAPSE

COMPETITOR
ADVERTISING

CATEGORY
OBSOLESCENCE

COMPETITOR
INNOVATION

BRAND-BUILDING

4.1 WHICH EXPERIENCES BUILD BRANDS?

In some companies, brand-building is the sole responsibility of the marketing team. The brand is seen as a consequence of advertising. However, this mode of thinking gets in the way. Every experience someone has in relation to a brand could influence how they think or feel about it. The mind doesn't discriminate between experiences curated by the marketing team and all other brand encounters. Customer experiences, for example, can be especially influential. They should all be consistent with the desired brand associations. A single good or bad experience with customer support services can have a big impact on future purchasing.

BRANDS ARE BUILT THROUGH ALL TOUCHPOINTS

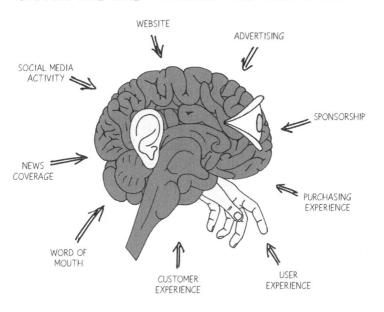

WEBSITE

ADVERTISING

SOCIAL MEDIA
ACTIVITY

SPONSORSHIP

NEWS
COVERAGE

PURCHASING
EXPERIENCE

WORD OF
MOUTH

CUSTOMER
EXPERIENCE

USER
EXPERIENCE

If all these experiences influence the brand, where should market-ers focus their limited resources? A great place to start is within the company. Great marketers inspire everyone to get involved in brand-building. They make employees believe in what the brand stands for. For example, it is said that when President John F. Kennedy first visited NASA, he met a janitor carrying a broom down the hallway. The president asked the workman what he did for NASA. The man replied, "I'm helping put a man on the Moon." With the whole organization behind the brand, the marketing team is off to a flying start.

Which touchpoints to prioritize depends on the brand's life stage.

NEW AND YOUNG BRANDS

With a few exceptions, new brands tend to have limited marketing budgets. Budgets only increase if the initial investment has been shown to deliver promising results. This means new brands can't opt for activities that cost a lot up front and take a long time to pay back. Brands in this situation are wise to focus on low-cost activities and use them cleverly to maximize their impact. For example, with a little creativity, news and social media can be enticed to share the brand's story (see the Lush example in *Section 6.3*). If you have an outstanding product or service, focus on obtaining testimonials from fans and then publicize them as widely as possible (e.g. via your social media channels and website, if you can afford it).

EXPANDING BRANDS

Invest in paid-for advertising when you have the budget to reach a sufficient number of your target consumers. Consider sponsorship if the cost per reach is attractive and if your goal is to build brand familiarity or appropriate associations from the sponsored property. In 2019, PayPal became a sponsor of the Football Association in the UK. Sponsoring the country's most popular sport helped PayPal to be seen as a trusted, everyday brand, giving it the credibility to compete with long-established brands such as VISA.

WELL-ESTABLISHED BRANDS

To maintain sales and profitability, well-established brands should continue to invest across multiple touchpoints. A big brand's share of advertising spend should be on a par with its share of the market (see *Section 4.5*). If it has ambitions for further growth, its share of spend needs to be higher. Paid-for advertising and sponsorship are good choices for maintaining a brand's saliency and reminding people what they like about the brand. Social media advertising also works well since the brand can leverage its distinctive assets to quickly trigger and reinforce existing brand memories.

4.2 THE ROLE OF PRODUCT INNOVATION

Product innovation means developing or buying new technologies or processes that enhance the user experience. Innovations can be used to upgrade existing products or launch superior new ones. Product innovation can contribute to brand success in four ways:

- User experience – ensuring the brand's delivery remains competitive
- Brand perceptions – reinforcing what makes the brand salient
- Category growth – creating new usage occasions and attracting new category users
- Brand extension – enabling growth by extending the brand into new areas

USER EXPERIENCE

In most categories, the user experience has a bigger influence on brand perceptions and repeat purchasing than other factors. Buyers have expectations about how a brand should deliver, based on its price and what it communicates about itself. In markets where alternative choices are readily available, people won't buy again if the product or service is disappointing. If you can innovate faster than your rivals, you will create a significant competitive advantage. If not, you'll need to match competitors' innovations quickly to avoid losing market share.

Online shoe and clothing retailer Zappos is famous for having built its brand by delivering a customer experience that is second to none. On its website, Zappos describes how it has leveraged social media and word of mouth to promote itself over the years, often making use of anecdotes that highlight its commitment to customer service excellence.

ZAPPOS CUSTOMER INTIMACY EXAMPLE

UNLIKE MOST ONLINE COMPANIES, ZAPPOS ACTIVELY ENCOURAGES PEOPLE TO CALL

INFORMATION

ENQUIRIES

CALLERS ARE GREETED BY FRIENDLY, HELPFUL, WELL-TRAINED PEOPLE, MOST OFTEN WITHIN JUST ONE MINUTE

COMPLAINTS

CUSTOMER INTERACTIONS

PURCHASING

THE SERVICE TEAM HAS NO SCRIPTS OR CALL-TIME LIMITS, AND CAN USE DISCRETION TO RESOLVE CUSTOMER ISSUES

CUSTOMER SUPPORT

CUSTOMERS CAN BUY ITEMS AND RETURN THEM WITHOUT ANY SHIPPING COSTS

THE CUSTOMER LOYALTY TEAM IS AVAILABLE 24-7-365, AND NEW TEAM MEMBERS ARE RECRUITED BASED ON THEIR COMPATIBILITY WITH THE COMPANY'S CUSTOMER-CENTRIC ETHOS

BRAND PERCEPTIONS

Strong brands come to mind readily when people are thinking about buying a category. Product innovation can help to strengthen the mental connections required for this to happen. Volvo, for example, commonly comes to people's minds when they are thinking about buying a family car and safety is a priority. Volvo has built its association with safety throughout its history. Volvo cars are safe because the company continually develops new safety features. In 1959, it introduced the three-point safety belt (and made it available to all car manufacturers despite owning the patent). In 2008, it introduced City Safety automatic braking. Volvo showcases these innovations in its advertising to reinforce people's perceptions of its safety and keep the brand top of mind.

CATEGORY GROWTH

According to an analysis of a billion shopping trips by Jared Schrieber (2021), brands that get people using the category for new usage contexts or bring new users tend to thrive. They grow the category and benefit most from its growth. Product innovation can be the key to achieving this. MP3 music players first appeared in 1997. The category didn't take off, however, until Apple entered the market. Apple launched its iPod in 2001, introducing a whole range of innovations. The iPod provided an easy way to transfer music from CDs, an intuitive user interface and access to thousands of songs via the iTunes store.

BRAND EXTENSION

Since launching the iPod, Apple has fuelled its meteoric growth by extending into new categories – most notably mobile phones. A strong innovation pipeline is essential for any brand seeking long-term growth. Dyson has become one of the world's most valuable brands by developing products that are functionally superior.

The company's founder, James Dyson, describes his approach to innovation in his book *Invention: A Life*. In 1974, Dyson invented the Ballbarrow – an innovative design that captured 50% of UK wheelbarrow sales. Superior products sell, but they only bring ongoing success if competitors can't copy them. Dyson learned this when a competitor raced a Ballbarrow me-too to market in the US and dominated sales in this much bigger region. Since then, Dyson has taken out over 6,000 patents to make its inventions hard to replicate. The brand's success stems from making products that are superior to alternatives in ways that consumers value and will pay more for. To achieve this, the company invests an estimated 15–20% of its revenue in research and development. It has over 1,000 engineers and scientists striving to refine and improve its products and stay ahead of the competition. The fact that Dyson products are also stylish and distinctive-looking enhances their appeal, helps them to command a premium price and makes it harder for competitors to imitate them without infringing copyright.

SOME OF DYSON PRODUCT INNOVATIONS

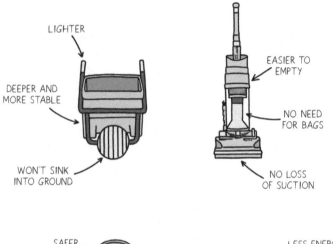

LIGHTER

DEEPER AND MORE STABLE

WON'T SINK INTO GROUND

EASIER TO EMPTY

NO NEED FOR BAGS

NO LOSS OF SUCTION

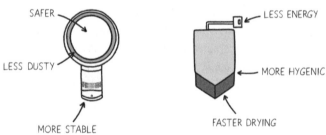

SAFER

LESS DUSTY

MORE STABLE

LESS ENERGY

MORE HYGENIC

FASTER DRYING

4.3 HOW TO LEVERAGE COMMUNICATIONS

The purpose of brand-building is to get more people to buy a brand and/or be prepared to pay more for it. Communications can help by bringing the brand to the top of people's minds when they are thinking about buying the category. They bias people's decisions in the brand's favour by evoking memories, thoughts and feelings. The more powerful, positive and relevant these are, the better.

The contribution communications need to make depends on the brand's circumstances. For little-known brands, the priority is to start building a rich set of mental associations. For well-established brands, the communication may only need to reinforce or refresh existing associations.

DIFFERENT ROLES FOR COMMUNICATIONS

SIMPLE PROPOSITION PEOPLE JUST NEED TO HEAR ABOUT	COMPLEX PROPOSITION REQUIRING SOME ELABORATION	BRAND NEEDS NEW ASSOCIATIONS TO APPEAL VS COMPETITORS	BRAND JUST NEEDS TO REINFORCE EXISTING ASSOCIATIONS	PEOPLE NEED TO BE PUSHED OVER THE LINE TO BUY
SHOUT	EXPLAIN	BUILD	REINFORCE	TRIGGER

The first four roles above are considered to be part of brand-building. The fifth one is known as activation or performance marketing. The nature of the task influences which media to use. Media such as cinema, TV and non-skippable YouTube lend themselves to forging new mental associations through storytelling. In-feed social advertising works well for quickly reinforcing existing associations since exposure durations are short.

The role of communications also depends on whether the brand delivers a strong user experience. Brands that deliver an exceptional experience and have built a passionate fanbase can thrive without investing heavily in advertising. Apple, GoPro, Rolls-Royce, Tesla and Trader Joe's are celebrated examples. These brands focus on leveraging brand advocacy (e.g. via social media). Even a brand that has grown well without much advertising can accelerate its growth through advertising. In 2009, Amazon CEO Jeff Bezos said: "Advertising is the price you pay for having an unremarkable product or service" (cited by Mello, 2021). Yet by 2022, Amazon had become the world's second biggest ad spender worldwide. The company had calculated the return it would achieve from advertising and determined that it was a great investment.

Based on the triangulation of evidence from a lifetime of experience, the author has concluded that:

> The pay-back from marketing communications is largest when it brings a great product to the attention of people who will appreciate it.

Communications cannot compensate for a poor product, at least not in the long term. Brand growth depends on the proportion of trialists who buy the brand again. This repurchase rate depends on how well the user experience lives up to expectations, especially in relation to the price paid. When the fruit-flavoured drink Sunny Delight was launched in the UK in 1998, it quickly became the country's third bestselling drink. Its initial success was thanks to a £10 million promotional campaign. The drink was sold in refrigerated cabinets and positioned as a healthier alternative to soft drinks. The product didn't, in fact, need refrigeration and contained 50g of sugar per serving. When the media brought these contradictions to consumers' attention, sales plummeted (see https://en.wikipedia.org/wiki/SunnyD).

Communications play their biggest role in categories where the user experience isn't highly differentiated or where emotions shape brand opinions more than product characteristics. Fragrances are a good example. Fragrance brands do have different aromas, but they have all been tested to make sure most people like how they smell. Whether someone buys Chanel or Givenchy is more to do with the associations that each brand triggers.

4.4 THE POWER OF PARTNERSHIP

It is easy to see why partnerships between brands are popular. If the brands' target audiences, goals and values are well aligned, partnerships are bound to be mutually beneficial. Advantages can include:

- Creating superior products
- Expanded reach – by pooling customer databases
- Strengthening each brand's mental presence and connotations by linking it with the other brand

The music industry leverages this approach all the time. A large proportion of tracks released as singles come from one artist but feature another. This results in fans of each artist hearing the track (e.g. on Spotify) and potentially checking out the other. The same thinking applies to all categories. If your brand could partner with another brand for mutual benefit, go for it!

Here are some examples of successful brand partnerships.

APPLE AND MASTERCARD

Apple and Mastercard teamed up to develop Apple Pay. Apple brought its huge user base of smartphone users and the expertise to create a slick user experience via iPhone and Apple Watch. Mastercard brought its worldwide network of retail partners. Apple Pay has become one of the world's most popular payment systems.

TACO BELL AND DORITOS

Taco Bell introduced the Doritos Locos Taco to its menu in 2012. It was a taco supreme with a special shell made from Doritos chips. The combination proved to be a big hit and is still on the menu today.

LEGO AND *STAR WARS*

The partnership between Lego and *Star Wars* started in 1999. Lego sets featuring *Star Wars* assets are among the company's bestsellers, thanks to the popularity of the *Star Wars* brand. In return, the owner of the *Star Wars* brand, Disney, takes a sizeable cut of the profits. According to Pymnts.com, Disney generated revenues of around $2 billion from the box office for *Star Wars: The Force Awakens*. It generated more than $6 billion from sales of related merchandise, including Lego sets and other toys, books, clothing and more.

BMW AND LOUIS VUITTON

The BMW i8 is a plug-in hybrid sports car that costs over £100,000 at the time of writing. BMW worked with luxury fashion brand Louis Vuitton to produce a luggage set designed specifically for the i8. As Louis Vuitton (2022) puts it: "They stack and fit together in an ingenious way in order to allow the driver to carry their most treasured possessions in style and security, without compromising the comfort and elegance of luxury travel." In other words, they fit neatly in the boot.

UBER AND SPOTIFY

The Uber–Spotify partnership allows Uber customers to decide what music to play on their journey as they wait for their ride to arrive. This enhances the user experience for Uber clients while highlighting the extensive range of music available from Spotify.

BETTY CROCKER AND HERSHEY'S

Betty Crocker makes a range of baking mixes. Since 2013, several of its mixes have included ingredients from the famous Hershey's range of candies.

4.5 HOW BRANDS CAN DIE

A single moment of indiscretion has the potential to ruin a brand. Gerald Ratner, chairman of the jewellery chain Ratners, was talking at an industry conference in 1991. During his speech, he revealed his contempt for some of Ratner's bestselling products. According to *BusinessBlogs*, when asked how his company was able to sell a sherry decanter for £4.95, Ratner said, "Because it's total crap." He went on to explain how they could sell a pair of earrings for under a pound: "They're cheaper than a shrimp sandwich from Marks and Spencer, but probably wouldn't last as long." His comments were widely reported in the press. Ratners had been the UK's largest jewellery chain, but within a few months it had disappeared from UK high streets. The 'Ratner effect' has become a warning to senior company managers. Leaders should only express opinions about their company's products if they are unambiguously positive.

Although brands can disappear overnight through reputational collapse, as in the example of Ratners, most fade away gradually as their category evolves.

HOW BRANDS CAN DIE

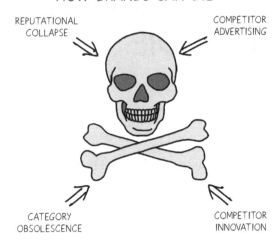

REPUTATIONAL
COLLAPSE

COMPETITOR
ADVERTISING

CATEGORY
OBSOLESCENCE

COMPETITOR
INNOVATION

COMPETITOR ADVERTISING

According to Les Binet and Peter Field (2013), brands need their share of advertising spend to be roughly in line with their share of the market in order to maintain their position. If a competitor has deeper pockets and invests much more in advertising than you can afford, your brand may struggle to survive. In these circumstances, the only option is to seek more funding. Your business leaders may need a clear explanation of why your brand is superior and why the long-term gain would be worth the investment.

COMPETITOR INNOVATION

If your competitors are coming up with innovations you cannot match, your brand will struggle to survive. New brands or strong brands from adjacent categories often represent the biggest threats. Mobile phones were first introduced by Motorola in 1973. Nokia became the market leader in 1998. It was the first brand to introduce games

(*Snake* in 1997) and wireless access to the internet (1999), and was an early adopter of 3G connectivity (2002). Since 2010, however, Apple and Samsung have competed for market dominance thanks to their superior technological advancements. For a brand to compete in a category with rapid innovation, it either needs to secure sufficient investment for research and development or find alternative areas on which to focus.

CATEGORY OBSOLESCENCE

When Netflix launched in 1998, it competed with Blockbuster by offering high-quality DVDs instead of VHS tapes. It provided a postal subscription service to avoid the expense of having physical stores. By 2001, DVD players had started to take off so Blockbuster launched its own DVD-by-mail service. But Blockbuster still had thousands of physical stores full of movies on VHS. This meant the company's costs, and hence the prices it needed to charge for rentals, were significantly higher than Netflix's. In 2007, Netflix launched an online streaming service. Blockbuster didn't. Within three years, Blockbuster filed for bankruptcy whereas Netflix went on to become one of the world's biggest brands. The VHS movie rental category became obsolete, replaced temporarily by DVDs and then by streaming. Blockbuster died because it didn't adapt quickly enough to consumer trends.

Companies with a portfolio of brands can compensate for the loss of revenue from struggling brands by investing profits in brands with more growth potential. Companies with a single brand will need to develop a new business strategy.

4.6 BRAND MIGRATION

There are times when a brand's name must change. This could be because of a dispute over legal ownership of the name. Or it could be to create alignment with a similar brand operating in other countries. Name changes need to be handled carefully. There is a risk that the familiarity and goodwill built by the brand over its lifetime could be thrown away. The goal of a brand migration should be to transfer as much of the brand's equity to its new name as possible.

OLIVIO BRAND MIGRATION

ORIGINAL PACKAGING

MIGRATION PHASE 1

MIGRATION PHASE 2

MIGRATION PHASE 3

Successful migrations usually involve a phased approach and advertising to communicate the change. UK plant-based spread Olivio was migrated to the international brand Bertolli in 2004. The author was an adviser to its parent company, Unilever, at the time. The transition went smoothly with no drop-off in sales.

Phase 1 involved communicating that Olivio was made from Bertolli olive oil. The message was featured on the pack and in Olivio's advertising. This helped to establish the Bertolli name and logo as a distinctive brand asset for Olivio (see *Chapter 3*). The more assets two brands have in common, the easier it is to migrate from one to the other without losing brand equity. The brand team came up with an ingenious idea for the start of Phase 2. For six weeks (approximately three buying cycles), a cardboard sleeve was put around the tubs. It had the same design as the pack from the previous phase. However, with the sleeve removed, the Phase 2 design was revealed. In other words, consumers themselves were part of the migration process. This helped to make the name change more memorable. At the same time, the brand used TV advertising to announce its new name. Phase 3 involved moving to a pack matching the design used in other countries. The migration lasted three years.

Other brands have used a similar, phased approach. Spanish bank Santander bought British bank Abbey in 2004. In 2005, Abbey started using Santander's flame logo and red colour in all its branches and advertising. Five years later, the name was switched. The rebrand was supported by a major TV advertising campaign featuring Formula 1 racing driver Lewis Hamilton.

CHAPTER 5

1894
1910
1950

LEVERAGING
CREATIVITY

5.1 MEMORABILITY

For advertising to have a brand-building effect, it needs to exert its influence a long time after the exposure. The best advertising continues to bias people's purchasing weeks, months and even years later. Consequently, the advertising needs to be memorable. The challenge for marketers is that very little of what people experience in daily life is important enough to be worth remembering. Let alone advertising. The human mind has a limited capacity for processing and storing information, so it must be selective in what it allows in. It is the ultimate 'walled garden,' carefully controlling access to the precious resources within its perimeter.

THE HUMAN MIND IS THE
ULTIMATE WALLED GARDEN

The human brain is a powerful organ that consumes a lot of energy. In the average adult, the brain consumes about 20% of the body's energy in a resting state (Jabr, 2012). We have therefore evolved our thinking processes to minimize unnecessary brain function – leaving us more energy to run away from sabre-toothed tigers and all the other life-preserving activities our ancestors needed to do.

The mind's gates are only unlocked if our senses detect something that might be worthy of our attention. Without us even realizing, our minds constantly analyse everything coming in from our senses. Our brain's 'central executive' automatically analyses our moment-by-moment experiences. It decides whether there is something that should be brought to our conscious attention and remembered for future reference.

The illustration below, based on the model proposed by Baddeley (2013), shows how the mind might process the experience of seeing a deer being hunted. Advertising will only be remembered if the central executive deems it sufficiently relevant.

OPERATIONS OF THE WORKING MEMORY

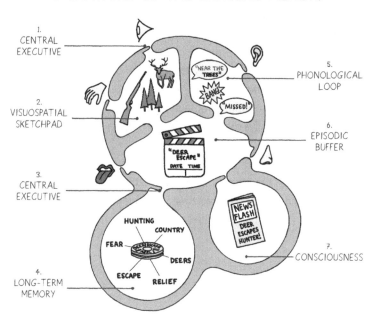

1. CENTRAL EXECUTIVE
2. VISUOSPATIAL SKETCHPAD
3. CENTRAL EXECUTIVE
4. LONG-TERM MEMORY
5. PHONOLOGICAL LOOP
6. EPISODIC BUFFER
7. CONSCIOUSNESS

1. CENTRAL EXECUTIVE
Determines which stimuli are worthy of attention and allowed into working memory

2. VISUOSPATIAL SKETCHPAD
Processes visual and tactile information to create an understanding of space and what's in it

3. CENTRAL EXECUTIVE
Determines whether experiences are delivered to consciousness and how they are stored in memory

4. LONG-TERM MEMORY
Memories of experiences are stored by connecting them to all relevant existing memories (so they can be retrieved later via various different triggers)

5. PHONOLOGICAL LOOP
Analyses speech and sound and allows the 'voice in our head' to help work out what we're experiencing

6. EPISODIC BUFFER
Determines the order in which things happened, i.e. how the 'story' unfolded

7. CONSCIOUSNESS
The mind processes lots of information without us being aware of it, and only experiences deemed 'important' by the central executive are made conscious

Memories do not include everything experienced by our senses – just edited highlights, or a fragmented montage. This is just enough to allow us to remember the incident and its meaning in case it is relevant in the future. The memory might include key images (the deer, the trees, the gun), sounds (the bang) and smells (the forest). It might also capture the feelings (fear, relief) and the meaning (close escape). The people who condense six hours of test match cricket footage into five minutes of highlights use a similar approach.

The challenge for advertisers is how to create something that will meet the central executive's relevance threshold, and how to ensure that the brand and the desired brand associations are included in the moments and ideas worth remembering.

5.2 DISTINCTIVENESS AND CREATIVITY

The first challenge for brand communications is to gain attention. If we paid attention to everything happening around us, our brains would soon become overloaded with information. To prevent this, we have evolved to ignore most of what's going on. Our unconscious brain uses our senses to constantly scan our environment using as little brainpower as possible. It only draws on precious conscious attention if it identifies something:

- Potentially dangerous
- Potentially rewarding
- Totally unfamiliar and worth checking out

It filters out everything else.

SCANNING FOR STIMULI WORTHY OF ATTENTION

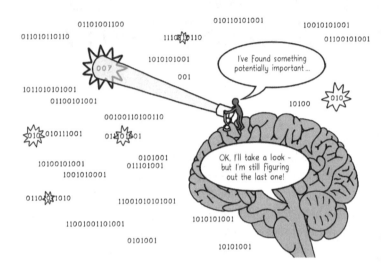

The 'cocktail party effect' illustrates how this works. At a party, we can hear multiple conversations going on at once, but we can choose to focus our conscious attention on the people we are talking to. However, our unconscious mind continues to scan all other sounds just in case. The roar of a lion, for example, would break through to our consciousness and so, indeed, would our name.

So, how can advertising break through the filtering process and gain attention?

According to the *World Heritage Encyclopaedia* (2018), sex was first used in advertising in 1871. Pearl Tobacco displayed an image of a 'naked maiden' on their cigarette packaging and sales rocketed. Sex is one of several topics humans find intrinsically attention-worthy.

WHAT WE PAY ATTENTION TO

WE ATTEND TO ANYTHING THAT STANDS OUT FROM THE ENVIRONMENT OR SEEMS OUT OF THE ORDINARY

in case it could be a threat,

an opportunity

or something to be wary of.

WE ARE ALSO PROGRAMMED TO PAY ATTENTION TO THINGS THAT ARE HIGHLY RELEVANT TO US PERSONALLY...

There are infinite ways for advertising to grab people's attention. Showing sexy people, babies or animals will usually work. But it is also possible to command attention by coming up with something distinctive and original.

If advertising has managed to grab people's attention, the next challenge is to hold their attention for as long as possible. This is where storytelling comes into its own. Telling a story is an effective way to communicate. Stories make it easier for people to take in and remember complex information and make it feel more important, credible and worth acting upon.

Whiskey brand Jack Daniel's excels at storytelling. The brand tells its origin story, starting in 1864, and the challenges it has faced since then, on its website and in its advertising. The anecdotes are interesting and memorable. They enhance the sense that the brand is authentic and of uncompromising quality.

Since 2009, the price comparison website Comparethemarket.com has run one of the most successful British ad campaigns ever. It features animated meerkat Aleksandr Orlov, the aristocratic Russian owner of the meerkat comparison site Comparethemeerkat.com. In the first ad, a frustrated Aleksandr tries to clear up the confusion between the two sites, directing people to Comparethemarket.com if they're actually looking for cheap insurance. The advertising, which was integrated across TV, Facebook, Twitter and the brand's websites, captured the public's imagination and produced immediate results thanks to sky-rocketing brand familiarity. According to *Campaign* magazine, the advertising had an immediate impact.

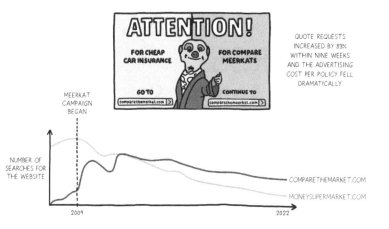

The catchphrase "Simples!" quickly entered the vernacular (it was finally added to the *Oxford English Dictionary* in 2019) and the soft toys of Aleksandr and his co-stars, which used to be given to customers when they took out policies, are highly collectable. Over the years, the campaign has been used to publicize a two-for-one cinema ticket promotion, launch the brand in Australia and promote AutoSergei, a service named after Aleksandr's techy sidekick, that automatically finds the best deals when policies are up for renewal.

5.3 CONSISTENCY ACROSS CHANNELS

It is well documented that advertising campaigns with a high degree of consistency across channels and executions are more effective. An analysis of entries to the 'Euro Effies' provides strong support for this. The Euro Effies are awards given to advertising campaigns for which there is compelling proof of their commercial impact. The campaigns are judged by a panel of independent experts. The Euro Effie organization gave the author access to its database of entries over five years. The goal was to identify common characteristics of the most effective campaigns. The analysis showed that the best predictor of campaign effectiveness was campaign consistency (Euro Effies, October 2016).

> The most effective campaigns have a high degree of thematic and aesthetic consistency across all campaign elements.

Some 53% of winning entries had this consistency compared to just 10% of entries that had insufficient evidence of a sales impact to reach the finals.

Consistency across campaign content has two benefits: synergy and memorability.

SYNERGY

If one element of a campaign succeeds in engaging an individual, they will be more likely to notice and pay attention to other elements. This works if the connection between the elements is obvious. The term 'lead ad' refers to content designed to establish a campaign as being worthy of attention in consumers' minds. Exposure to lead ads is believed to cause other elements to be more effective than they would have been if used in isolation. Lead ads enhance campaign performance more if they are used early on and appear in channels that 'force' exposure, such as YouTube (non-skippable), TV or video on demand.

MEMORABILITY

Having an established set of distinctive brand assets makes it easier for the audience to link campaign elements together (see *Section 3.2*). The success of Red Bull (see *Section 2.6*) illustrates the value of consistency across channels. The gin brand Hendrick's is another great example. It built a strong brand identity by conveying a coherent aesthetic via every touchpoint. Launched in 1999, Hendrick's initial growth was modest. Sales took off when it introduced a distinctive 'brand world' inspired by its apothecary-style packaging. Hendrick's now uses the same visual style, tone of voice and narrative themes everywhere. An obsessive interest in cucumbers is one of the brand's motifs.

Paid-for advertising, point-of-sale displays, websites, social media activities and promotional events all play their part.

THE DISTINCTIVE BRAND WORLD OF HENDRICK'S

BOTANICAL
BOTTLES

INSPIRED
INGREDIENTS

MANICURED
MOUSTACHES

CURIOUS
CONTRAPTIONS

PECULIAR
PROPAGANDA

ECCENTRIC
ENTERPRISES

EXTRAORDINARY
EXPERIENCES

By 2017, Hendrick's had become one of only eight gin brands to sell more than a million cases worldwide.

5.4 CONSISTENCY OVER TIME

Memories become stronger and longer lasting if they are reinforced repeatedly over time, rather than coming from a single, concentrated period of exposure. Cramming for exams, for example, can boost a student's scores a little, but it doesn't help them to remember the concepts for long (National Research Council, 1994). The same is true for advertising. Ideas, specific sounds, images and so on work their way into our long-term memory best if they are featured in a brand's advertising year after year. *Section 3.4* highlights how many leading brands have successfully used the same distinctive brand assets in their advertising for decades.

It is better to evolve existing distinctive brand assets over time, to keep them feeling contemporary, than to replace them with new ones. The Michelin Man, Tony the Tiger and even Mickey Mouse have changed significantly over the years, but they have always remained easy to recognize.

MICHELIN MAN OVER THE YEARS

1894   1910   1950

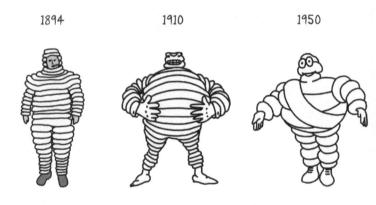

Moving away from well-established brand assets can cause major problems.

In 2002, PG Tips moved away from using chimps in its advertising. The brand team told the author that it wanted to stop using chimps because of growing public concern over animal exploitation, as well as their own reservations. The campaigns that followed struggled with brand linkage. The connection between PG Tips and chimps had been forged throughout most viewers' lifetimes. This made it hard for new advertising styles to become associated with the brand. The branding issue of the campaign that followed could have been avoided if it had featured animated chimps rather than birds.

The value of long-established brand assets applies to packaging too. In 2009, fruit juice brand Tropicana made changes to its pack design. The original pack showed an orange with a striped straw in it below the brand's familiar logo. The new design was radically different. It showed orange juice in a glass and a new logo that was written vertically. The change resulted in an immediate drop in sales of 20% that cost the company $30 million before they went back to the original design (*The Branding Journal*, 2022). The sales decline was believed to be because buyers struggled to find their usual brand in store, which triggered them to try other brands. Disruptions to buying behaviour are not desirable, especially if other brands offer better user experiences for their price.

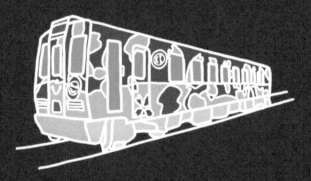

CHAPTER 6

LEVERAGING
MEDIA

6.1 BRAND-BUILDING MEDIA

The best media for brand-building give the content a chance to hold people's attention long enough to tell a story. It takes, perhaps, six seconds to tell a simple story and 30 seconds to tell one that's emotionally powerful. True creativity, however, can trump these rules of thumb.

Here's a story, conveyed using just one visual and four words at a bus stop. Its effectiveness relies, to some extent, on knowing that Specsavers is a brand of opticians. The fact that the catchphrase was already well established only enhanced the ad's effectiveness.

OUTDOOR STORYTELLING

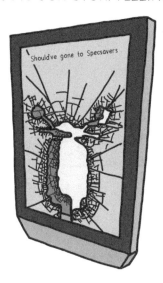

TV, video on demand, cinema and non-skippable YouTube are especially effective for brand-building. When people are exposed to the advertising in these media, they are relaxing, simply waiting for their chosen content to start. In the case of magazines, they are browsing the articles and the ads until something captures their imagination. When consuming these channels, people are 'captive'. They are not trying to achieve something else. This means they tend to watch the advertising for at least a few seconds. These channels keep about a third of the audience engaged for at least six seconds, which is just enough to tell a simple but memorable story about a brand (Ebiquity, 2021). The best content, however, is so compelling that some people watch it for even longer – especially on TV. The Ebiquity report shows how attention varies by media channel. The results are based on eye-tracking data provided by Lumen.

DWELL TIMES BY MEDIA

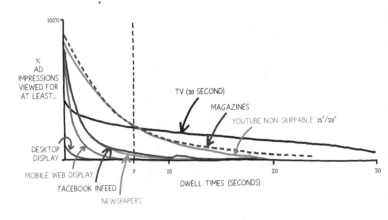

Telling stories (see *Section 5.2*) is a good way of holding people's attention for a long time. After all, who doesn't want to know what happens at the end of a story? Start telling an intriguing story in the first few seconds and you'll keep lots of people until the end.

6.2 SALES ACTIVATION MEDIA

Social media in-feed advertising and digital display are best suited to sales activation because their exposure durations are short. As people scroll through their social media feed, they tend to race past the advertising. They only slow down when they find content that interests them – posts from family members or friends, for example. The viewer has full control over how long they spend watching the advertising. This explains why the average exposure duration for social in-feed and digital display advertising is just 1.5 seconds (Ebiquity, 2021). This is similar to the dwell times achieved by most outdoor media, such as posters and billboards.

AVERAGE EYES-ON DWELL TIME BY MEDIUM

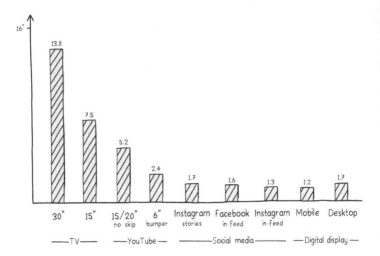

If consumers are already predisposed to a brand, short-exposure ads that bring the brand to the forefront of their mind can be effective. They remind people of what they like about the brand, trigger a purchase or at least encourage people to find out more about the brand. Media that deliver short exposures are not well suited, however, to brand-building. It is difficult to tell a memorable story in just one or two seconds.

HARNESSING EARNED MEDIA

Earned media comprises messages about a brand generated outside the company. It includes product reviews, mentions in the press, by bloggers or on TV programmes, and comments made by individuals on social media or face to face.

Market research firm Nielsen conducted a survey of 30,000 people across 60 countries in 2015. The research revealed that opinions from third parties are more credible and impactful than advertising claims. In some categories, customer reviews and ratings on Amazon and Trustpilot can be hugely influential. Any brand with a following of passionate advocates is well placed to harness the power of earned media. The trick is to provide fans with opportunities to express their love for the brand. Then share these positive endorsements far and wide.

Toiletries brand Lush has made the most of earned media. Since launching in 1995, it has grown its annual revenues to over £1.3 billion (ReferralCandy, 2019). Lush sells high-price, cruelty-free, eco-friendly, handmade cosmetics described as 'fresh' and displayed in the style of a greengrocer. To promote its differentiated and distinctive brand, Lush has focused on social media. Until 2021, the brand posted regularly on platforms including Facebook,

Twitter and Instagram. At the same time, it inspired its fan base to generate and share its own content. Lush creates in-store experiences and news stories that are ideal for sharing. For most brands, this would be a risky strategy. Yet Lush succeeded in reaching millions of consumers on a regular basis.

LUSH EARNED MEDIA EXAMPLE

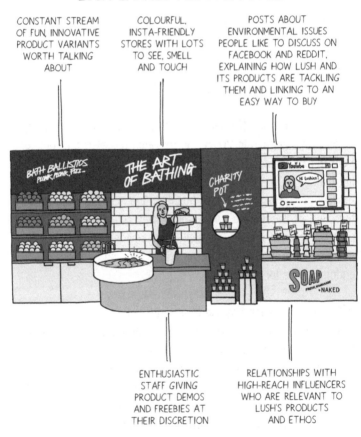

CONSTANT STREAM OF FUN, INNOVATIVE PRODUCT VARIANTS WORTH TALKING ABOUT

COLOURFUL, INSTA-FRIENDLY STORES WITH LOTS TO SEE, SMELL AND TOUCH

POSTS ABOUT ENVIRONMENTAL ISSUES PEOPLE LIKE TO DISCUSS ON FACEBOOK AND REDDIT, EXPLAINING HOW LUSH AND ITS PRODUCTS ARE TACKLING THEM AND LINKING TO AN EASY WAY TO BUY

ENTHUSIASTIC STAFF GIVING PRODUCT DEMOS AND FREEBIES AT THEIR DISCRETION

RELATIONSHIPS WITH HIGH-REACH INFLUENCERS WHO ARE RELEVANT TO LUSH'S PRODUCTS AND ETHOS

In November 2021, Lush announced that it would close its accounts on Facebook, Instagram, TikTok and Snapchat because of concerns over the content that users of these networks are exposed to. If Lush manages to maintain its strong brand through user testimonials and earned media, this decision could act as an example for other brands. If not, the brand may suffer from not using media channels that have served it well previously.

6.4 COMBINING MEDIA

There are two considerations when choosing which media you should use to promote your brand:

- What combination of media will reach as many category users as possible?
- Do you have a mix of media good at brand-building and sales activation?

MAXIMIZING REACH

Extensive research by the Ehrenberg-Bass Institute has shown that brand penetration is a much stronger indicator of brand size than brand loyalty (Sharp, 2010). Brands within the same category are largely interchangeable and long-term growth is better achieved by reaching a mass audience rather than targeting a niche. The media environment has become fragmented; no single medium can reach everyone in the target audience. A multi-media approach is needed. Jasper Snyder and Manuel Garcia-Garcia (2016) found that returns on media investment are higher if more channels are used.

USING MULTIPLE MEDIA INCREAES ROI

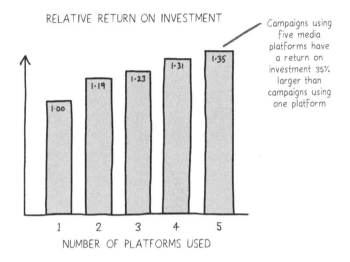

RELATIVE RETURN ON INVESTMENT

Campaigns using five media platforms have a return on investment 35% larger than campaigns using one platform

1·00 1·19 1·23 1·31 1·35

1 2 3 4 5

NUMBER OF PLATFORMS USED

The enhanced effectiveness may be because using multiple media helps to increase a campaign's total reach. It might also be because savvy advertisers combine brand-building and activation advertising, leveraging the channels that are suited to each task.

COMBINING BRAND-BUILDING AND SALES ACTIVATION

Les Binet and Peter Field (2013) found that spending on average 60% of the media budget on brand-building and 40% on sales activation maximized profit.

BALANCING BRAND BUILDING
AD SALES ACTIVATION

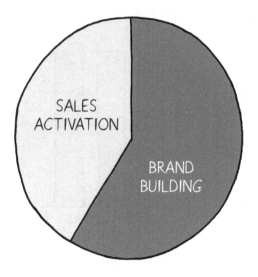

However, Binet and Field explain that the 60:40 ratio is only a guide. The optimum combination varies by brand. A brand with effective brand-building advertising and weak activation might do best to invest more in brand-building, and vice versa. The right ratio depends on the brand's strengths and weaknesses versus competitors.

CHANGES IN BRAND EQUITY VS CHANGES IN MARKET SHARE

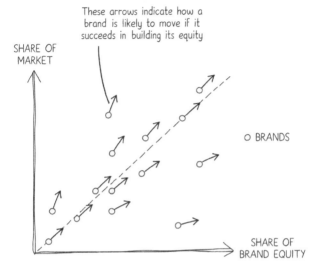

If a brand has built strong equity but struggles to translate this into sales, further brand-building may have little effect – hence the shallow incline of the arrows below the line in the illustration above. A brand with weak equity but relatively strong sales, on the other hand, is likely to respond well to brand-building – hence the steep gradient of brands above the line.

Market research can help to identify which strategy is likely to be more effective (see *Section 7.3*). Brands above the line in the graph above respond more to brand-building advertising. Brands below the line respond less to enhanced brand equity and more to changes in factors such as distribution or pricing.

6.5 EXPLOITING EACH MEDIUM'S UNIQUE STRENGTHS

Choosing the right media for your brand is a complex decision. Different media are suited to different brand objectives. Certain media, including cinema, TV and radio, enhance brand credibility – especially if the advertising is on a network with a reputation for quality content. Outdoor advertising can also have this effect, provided it is in appealing locations. Canadian philosopher Marshall McLuhan (1964) said that "the medium is the message." He was right that a brand's choice of media affects how people perceive it and the effectiveness of the advertising. These effects have been proven by Eun Sook Known and colleagues (2018).

Beyond reaching the target audience cost-effectively, the most effective media channels for a brand:
- Generate high audience involvement
- Are highly regarded by their audience
- Have content that is relevant to the category or what the brand stands for

An ad for a performance at the Metropolitan Opera will be more effective if it is placed in the broadsheet *The New York Times* than in the tabloid *The New York Post*. The former has a more affluent readership and features advertising for prestigious brands. Advertising in this esteemed publication will elevate the brand's status, helping it to command a price premium. A luxury brand's reputation could even be damaged if it were to promote itself via the wrong channels.

Each medium has its own strengths:

- **TV**, **cinema** and **non-skippable YouTube** are best suited to long-form video advertising that tells a memorable story about the brand.
- **Radio advertising** tends to reach people when they are engaged in another activity requiring very little of their attention (e.g. while driving, relaxing, cooking, eating or drinking, or doing the housework). This means that advertising messages have a good chance of breaking through. Listeners tend to be on their own and in their own homes or cars, so radio is ideal for conveying intimate messages.
- **Out-of-home advertising** can make people feel that a brand is contemporary and relevant. For example, KitKat decorated trains from Tokyo taking students off to university. It used a blossom design, which symbolizes good luck in Japan.

KITKAT LUCKY TRAIN

- **Sponsorship** is ideal for increasing brand name awareness and enhancing credibility. It strengthens brand appeal among people who love the sponsored property. Rolex has sponsored TED Talks since 2008 to connect with the affluent, intelligent audience that watches these videos.
- **Specialist magazines and websites** provide a good way to reach audiences that are most relevant to a brand. People use these media because they have specific interests, so the most effective advertising is tailored to these interests.
- **Magazines** and **some outdoor media** allow people to use their phones to find out more about a product via QR codes. This is ideal for brands with a unique and highly relevant consumer proposition.
- People usually see **social in-feed advertising** when they are using their phones. This provides an opportunity to trigger an immediate sale (e.g. by linking to an e-commerce platform). Social ads can also contribute to brand-building but only if they are able to engage people for long enough to leave a lasting memory about the brand.

Brands can also make their advertising more memorable by choosing channels that convey the their message in a memorable way. For example, Bic built giant models of its razors and placed them in fields of grass alongside busy roads in Japan. This created a powerful mental image, reinforcing the brand's efficacy.

BIC RAZOR EXAMPLE

CHAPTER 7

BRAND MEASUREMENT

7.1 IDENTIFYING YOUR KPIS

To manage your brand well, you will need to establish a set of key performance indicators, or KPIs. You and your colleagues must feel confident that the chosen metrics link to business success. They should include measures of physical availability, mental availability, behavioural sales drivers and user satisfaction.

Measures of physical availability include:
- Distribution
- Visibility in retail stores and/or on websites
- Visibility when people search for the category
- Uptake of the brand's mobile app
- Price acceptability

Those for mental availability include:
- Category-prompted spontaneous brand mentions and/or net mentions across the main category usage contexts
- Purchase consideration rating and/or ratings of how positive people feel towards the brand, how relevant it is to their needs, how unique it seems, whether it sets category trends (or similar)
- Levels of search for the brand (vs competitors)
- Mentions of the brand and/or uploads of pictures including the brand on social media (vs competitors)

Behavioural drivers of sales might encompass:
- Footfall per store and/or web traffic (or similar)
- Levels of first-time trials and/or acquisitions
- Annual penetration (size of customer base)
- Repeat purchase and/or retention rate (vs expected rate given the brand's size)

Finally, user satisfaction might be measured through:
- Overall opinion in user testing (vs competitors)
- Feedback from mystery shoppers (people pretending to be shoppers, who report back on their experiences)
- Average review scores (vs competitors)
- Numbers of users accessing troubleshooting services

To set KPIs, you need a good understanding of what drives success in your category and the business strategy that will enable your brand to thrive.

Consider a fast-food chain that has grown for decades by opening restaurants across a country. At some point, the brand will reach a ceiling in terms of physical availability. Future growth will depend on getting more people to visit its existing restaurants and/or getting them to visit for a wider variety of needs and occasions. For example, if people rarely visit the restaurant to have a coffee, an effective growth strategy might be to target coffee drinking by advertising the high quality, variety or value of the coffees it offers.

COME TO US FOR COFFEE

The KPIs for the campaign might include:

- The proportion of restaurants offering the product
  (an 'operational KPI')
- Footfall per restaurant per day
  (a 'consumer behaviour KPI')
- Mentions of the brand when consumers are asked:
  "Which brands come to mind when you're thinking of
  having a coffee break?"
  (a 'brand KPI')

7.2 CALIBRATING YOUR KPIS

Brand and consumer behaviour KPIs need to be calibrated before they can be used to guide marketing decisions. Marketers need to know two things:

- How changes in KPIs translate into profit
- The investment that would be required to achieve these changes

These estimates are essential to produce a compelling business case.

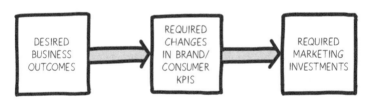

They also allow marketers to illustrate the consequences of reducing the marketing budget.

Marketing mix modelling, also known as sales modelling, is a statistical approach to estimating the relationships highlighted in the illustrations above. It is based on what a specific brand has experienced historically. At least two years' worth of weekly back data is needed. Some models include brand and consumer KPIs. Others quantify the relationship between marketing investments and business outcomes directly. Including brand and consumer KPIs helps the model to interpret the data patterns more accurately. It also provides clearer insights into how to achieve target business outcomes.

If you don't have the data you need to develop your own model, you can use results from other brands to estimate the relationships. Market research companies and academics publish aggregated data that provides an indication of what a brand might achieve from its investments. For example, Dominique Hanssens has compiled results from hundreds of academic studies. He has established how changes in marketing spend typically translate into business outcomes. On average, a 1% change in spend on efforts to increase distribution results in a sales change of between 0.6% and 1.7%. For sales calls, the sales change is 0.3%. For advertising, it is 0.1% for an average established brand. However, this can increase to 0.9% for new brands or strong new products from established brands (Pauwels et al., 2004).

These ratios are called 'sales elasticities.' To determine which activities are the best value for your brand, you need to estimate their elasticities and compare their costs.

If you have access to the necessary data, developing a marketing mix model for your brand is usually worth the time and money.

Including brand and consumer behaviour metrics within the model makes it even more useful. It will tell you which brand and consumer KPIs have the biggest impact on your business outcomes and which elements of the marketing mix to focus on. A sophisticated sales model reveals the relationships between marketing investments, brand and consumer KPIs, and business outcomes.

MARKET MIX AND BRAND MODEL EXAMPLE

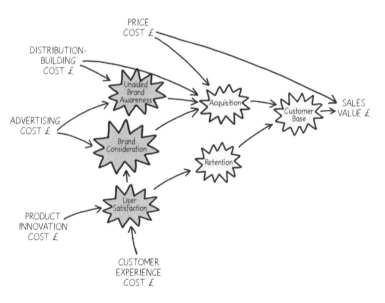

If the relevant data is available, additional 'driver analyses' can make the marketing task clearer. These analyses identify the specific brand perceptions that drive brand consideration most effectively and which aspects of the user experience have the greatest influence on satisfaction.

OPTIMIZING YOUR RETURN

Estimates of the commercial return from marketing activities are usually based on what has happened in the past. They assume the activity will be of average quality. This makes sense when marketers are preparing a business case. After all, there is no guarantee the work will be exceptional. On the other hand, when marketers are developing activity, they should strive to beat the odds by producing work that is outstandingly effective. This requires creativity and originality. Market research can also make a big difference, provided it is used wisely.

PRODUCT INNOVATION

The role of market research in product development is often denigrated. Henry Ford, who created the first mass market car company, is reported to have said: "If I had asked people what they wanted, they would have said faster horses." Although he may not have actually said this (Vlaskovits, 2011), even if he did, market research has moved on since the 1900s. Modern research identifies which aspects of the user experience people would appreciate most. It doesn't expect consumers to invent a solution. Back in the 1900s, consumers would have talked about what was wrong with horse-powered, long-distance travel: the lengthy duration, discomfort, feeling of insecurity and high cost.

These issues were all addressed when the Ford Model-T launched in 1908.

Modern research serves two roles:
- It establishes whether a new product concept has potential and is worth progressing
- It identifies the features that matter most to consumers so that the final product is as relevant and appealing as possible

Sadly, most new products fail. *Harvard Business Review* has reported that 75% of retail products fail in their first year (Schneider and Hall, 2011). Increasing the odds delivers a significant commercial advantage. Improvements made thanks to research give products a better chance of success in the market. Asking four or five people for their opinions might provide useful soundbites, but more extensive research (e.g. at least 200 people) is needed to guide strategy.

ADVERTISING DEVELOPMENT

When it comes to advertising, market research can play a huge role in making sure the final executions are effective. The strongest advertising:
- Grabs people's attention by being out of the ordinary or triggering a strong instinctive reaction
- Holds people's attention by telling a story and/or providing a spectacle for the senses
- Creates connections in people's memories that help the brand spring to mind when they think about buying the category

Chapter 5 explains in more detail why these criteria are important. Market research can measure how well potential advertising stacks up against them. It provides insights on how to improve advertising.

Feedback on early prototypes at each stage of the advertising development process helps in three ways:
- It highlights the most promising themes and storylines
- It identifies how to bring the core messages to life in the most engaging way
- It prevents the creative team from veering off in the wrong direction

It is good practice to get feedback at each stage of the advertising development process using prototypes. This keeps the creative team on track and ensures the end result will resonate well. Research feedback isn't always essential. But developing and deploying a big-budget campaign without it is risky. Investing a small proportion of your media budget in research shows accountability to your company's owners. It also helps to maximize the return from your production and media costs.

Some advertisers believe consumer feedback stifles creativity and undervalues groundbreaking ideas. The author's experience is that feedback tends to help much more than hinder. But the creative team and researchers must have a shared understanding of what makes effective advertising. When they do, magic can happen. Guinness's "Surfer" ad from 1999 dominates polls for 'best ad ever.' According to Michael Harvey, global consumer planning director at Guinness at the time, research was part of the ad's success:

> [The research] has not in any way suppressed Guinness's legendary creativity. Indeed, the famous "Surfer" ad went through research in animatic form [hand-drawn/simply animated], was enhanced as a result, and went on to its place in advertising history.

Cadbury's 2007 ad "Gorilla" might never have been aired if it hadn't been for the positive feedback from consumers. According to Phil Rumbol, marketing director for Cadbury at the time, the ad was initially not well received by the business: "It was seen by many within the company as nonsense," he admits. After six months of debate about whether to air the ad, market research provided the necessary reassurance (Choueke, 2012). Rachel Barrie, strategy director at Fallon, Cadbury's creative agency, explained:

> Millward Brown [a leading advertising research company] had to recalibrate its own scale to measure how engaging and impactful it was. The thing that it failed on was its 'persuasion test' but Millward Brown said we should still run the ad.

7.4 GUIDING COURSE-CORRECTIONS

Section 2.3 explains how to identify the usage contexts your brand should aim to dominate in consumers' minds in order to grow. If your analysis and judgement are sound, and your marketing activity is strong, your brand should enjoy a period of growth. However, things don't always go to plan. It's important to check that your brand is developing as intended and, if it isn't, to determine why not.

A brand tracking research programme will highlight when course correction is required:

BRAND TRACKING PROGRAMMES

ELEMENT	PURPOSE	METHOD	FREQUENCY
Brand tracking	Check progress vs brand KPIs (see Section 7.2)	Surveys	E.g. quarterly
Consumer tracking	Check progress vs consumer KPIs (see Section 7.2)	Subscription to syndicated category data (or from brand tracking)	E.g. quarterly
Retail tracking	Check distribution levels, promotional activity & selling price vs competitors	Subscription to syndicated category data (if available)	E.g. quarterly
Search levels	Monitor levels of interest in your brand over time vs competitors	Google Trends	E.g. quarterly
Website traffic	Monitor number of visits to your website	Your web-hosting service or Google Analytics	E.g. quarterly
Marketing mix modelling	Estimate the return on investment from different marketing activities	Statistical analysis relating levels of spend, brand and consumer KPIs, and commercial outcomes such as sales	E.g. annual
Brand equity deep-dive	Check if category or brand drivers have changed; assess strength of distinctive brand assets	Survey	E.g. every 1-2 years (more often for dynamic categories)
Trend review	Establish which emotional needs & product features are becoming more/less important to category users	Analysis of Google Trends; subscription to relevant trends reports (if available)	E.g. every 1-2 years (more often for dynamic categories)

Sales data on its own is not enough to enable the right decisions to be made. Sales are affected by many factors, making it hard to isolate the effect of the branding strategy. Also, a new brand strategy often takes time to start exerting its impact on sales (see *Section 1.4*). Brand tracking provides early indicators of whether a new brand strategy is working or if an established strategy is losing efficacy.

BRAND TRACKING

A brand-tracking survey should include these questions or equivalents:

- Which brands of *category* can you think of? ('Unaided brand awareness')
- Which of these brands [show logos] have you heard of? ('Aided brand awareness')
- Which have you ever bought?
- Which have you bought most recently?
- If you were buying *category*, how strongly would you consider *brand* [show scale, e.g. very strongly, quite strongly, might or might not consider, probably would not consider, definitely would not consider]?
- Which of these brands [show logos] do you associate with [target usage contexts]?
- Which of these brands [show logos] have you seen advertised recently?

Data from a survey along these lines can answer a range of brand management questions such as the ones outlined below.

Q1. Is branding important in our category now?

If the data looks like this ...

If the data looks like this ...

The answer is YES.

People tend to buy brands they are more predisposed towards.

The answer is NO.

People consider some brands slightly more strongly but often buy other brands anyway (e.g. because of availability or price).

Even if branding has little influence on purchasing today, it might still offer a growth opportunity. Your brand might gain a competitive advantage by explaining why people should care about which brand they buy. Before the "Intel Inside" campaign launched in 1991, most PC buyers wouldn't have given any thought to the make of a machine's microprocessor. Intel soon changed this. Its own advertising showcased the speed and reliability of its technology. The company also partnered with respected PC brands. Intel charged its partners 6% less for its components. In return, PC manufacturers put an "Intel Inside" sticker on their products and included a short audio-visual ident within their advertising. The PC manufacturers were more than happy with the arrangement. Besides the cost saving, they soon found that they could charge 10% more for their PCs if they contained Intel's technology.

Any brand that is functionally superior to alternatives has the opportunity to command a price premium and grow through advertising. This applies even if the category is currently seen as a commodity. The strategy is particularly effective if the brand can sustain its superiority via innovation, never allowing competitors to catch up.

Q2. Should we focus on brand-building at the moment?

If the data looks like this ...

The answer is YES.

Purchasing levels are high relative to consideration indicating that a focus on brand-building should work well.

If the data looks like this ...

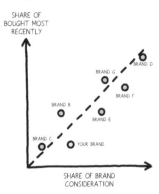

The answer is NO.

Your brand's existing consideration isn't being converted into purchasing. Focus on operational basics ahead of brand-building for now.

If your brand already enjoys high sales relative to its level of consideration, it must have established strong distribution and a price that consumers are happy with. If so, marketing activities designed to make the brand more appealing are likely to work well. Brands that struggle to sell despite relatively high levels of consideration should address their distribution and pricing challenges before investing in brand-building. See *Section 6.4* for how to combine media depending on where your brand sits on this cross-plot.

Q3. Is our advertising getting our brand noticed?

If the data looks like this ...

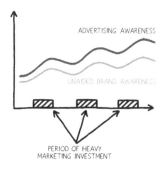

The answer is YES.

Unaided brand and advertising awareness are responding well.

If the data looks like this ...

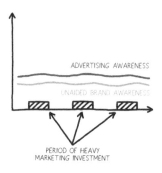

The answer is NO.

The advertising lacks impact or consumers aren't remembering the brand.

If unaided brand and advertising awareness show long-term growth, your marketing investment is helping to grow your brand. You can compare the uplifts achieved by your activity, per dollar invested, with competitors or wider benchmarks. This helps you to determine whether your activity is as strong as it could be. If it isn't, you may need to look for other partners able to produce more effective activity.

Q4. Is our advertising communicating as intended?

If the data looks like this ...

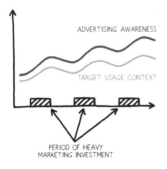

The answer is YES.

Increases in ad awareness mirror
increases in the brand's association
with targeted usage context(s).

If the data looks like this ...

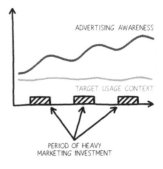

The answer is NO.

The advertising is getting the brand
noticed but not associating it with
the target usage context(s).

If your advertising is communicating as intended, you would expect
to see increases in ad awareness and target brand associations
in line with advertising spend. If ad awareness increases but this
doesn't translate into the desired impressions, your advertising may
be keeping your brand salient, but not working exactly as intended.

Q5. Is our brand getting stronger?

If the data looks like this ...

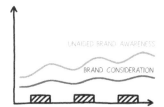

If the data looks like this ...

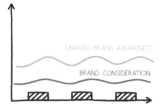

The answer is YES.

Both of the brand KPIs are growing in the long term.

The answer is NO.

KPIs respond to periods of heavy marketing investment, but there is no long-term build.

Long-term growth in unaided brand awareness and brand consideration signals that your brand is becoming increasingly prominent and appealing. If these measures respond to heavy spend but keep falling back to the same level afterwards, you probably need to spend more to develop more effective advertising content.

Q6. Is our brand's strength translating into purchasing?

If the data looks like this ...

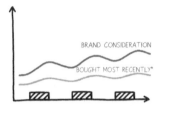

If the data looks like this ...

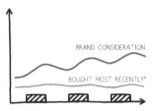

* FOR YOUNG BRANDS: EVER BOUGHT

The answer is YES.

As brand consideration grows,
purchasing follows.

The answer is NO.

More people are considering the
brand, but they are not buying it.
Low availability, high price or weak
sales activation might be the problem.

This relates to question two above. If increases in brand strength
are not translating into purchasing, you may need to work on your
operational basics first.

Q7. Should we continue with our messaging strategy?

If the data looks like this ...   If the data looks like this ...

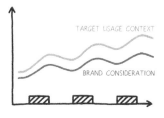

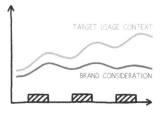

The answer is YES.

Consideration continues to grow as more people associate the brand with the target usage context.

The answer is NO.

The approach worked initially, but the usage context may have become less relevant or its ceiling may have been reached.

If brand consideration is no longer responding as anticipated, you can use Google Trends to shed light on the issue. If searches related to the brand's target usage occasion(s) are declining, the topic must be becoming less relevant to consumers. If so, it may be time to refocus communications on a different usage context.

CONCLUSION

Branding is not a cure-all. It won't help a business with fundamental problems. A strong brand 'nudges' people towards your products and services. It cannot compensate for a poor product. It makes little difference if your product is hard to find or over-priced. Branding is only a good investment when you have something worth selling and easily available.

For some organizations, branding isn't a priority. A company that dominates its industry due to its scale, for example, could grow by expanding its strong operational model. Cost advantages in manufacturing and distribution might inhibit competitors. If so, branding is may not be worthwhile. In any competitive market, however, branding is one of the best investments a company can make. Building a strong brand has become as important as delivering a good product. It can mean the difference between success and failure. Product innovations can be copied. Brands cannot.

Once established, a brand with a rich set of positive mental connections provides its owners with major commercial benefits. It is the value that a brand brings to the business that shareholders care about.

Benefits include:
- Better opportunity for revenue growth
- Ability to charge more and maximize profits
- Improved odds of success for new products and services
- Greater receptivity from potential investors
- Better employee satisfaction and retention
- Superior calibre job applicants
- Protection from competitive pressure
- Resilience in an economic downturn

Yet it takes time and money before a company can enjoy these benefits. Marketers need to present the potential gain from brand-building in a compelling way. Businesses need to treat branding as a long-term investment and plan their finances accordingly. Stakeholders need to be patient in waiting for the returns that brand-building will bring. They should also insist on businesses leveraging consumer insights and data. This ensures brand-building investments are being well used.

The world's most successful brands understand what existing and future brands care about. They use this insight to shape every element of the marketing mix. By doing this, they build brands that people are happy to buy and pay more for. They introduce new products and services that make life easier or more rewarding. They promote them using communications that inform, entertain and enrich people's everyday lives.

If you want to build a brand like this, use the advice outlined in *The Branding Book*:

1. Establish what your buyers and potential buyers care about
2. Review trends to predict how consumers' priorities might evolve
3. Learn how people currently see your brand, its competitors and wider alternatives
4. Develop a clear vision for what you want to connect with your brand in consumers' minds
5. Choose a set of distinctive brand assets and feature them at every opportunity across all consumer touchpoints
6. Use originality and creativity to forge the desired mental connections cost-effectively
7. Invest enough to ensure your brand comes to mind on a par with or ahead of competitors when people are thinking about buying the category
8. Aim to reach as many relevant people as your budget allows
9. Ensure your brand is brought to mind close to the point of sale, when people are deciding which brand to buy
10. Use consumer research and data to monitor progress and highlight when course correction is needed

By following these ten principles, you will build a brand that's cherished by consumers and company stakeholders alike.

BIBLIOGRAPHY

Aaker, David A., and Erich Joachimsthaler. "The Brand Relationship Spectrum: The Key to the Brand Architecture Challenge." *California Management Review* 42, no. 4 (2000): 8–23.

Aaker, David. "How Pampers made Diapers Relevant in China." *Prophet.com*. Last modified n.d., https://www.prophet.com/2013/05/how-pampers-made-diapers-relevant-in-china

Argo, Jennifer J., Monica Popa and Malcolm C. Smith. "The Sound of Brands." *Journal of Marketing* 74, no. 4 (2010): 97–109.

Baddeley, Alan. *Essentials of Human Memory (Classic Edition)*. Abingdon-on-Thames: Routledge, 2013.

Ben-Hafaïedh, Cyrine, and Anaïs Hamelin. "Questioning the Growth Dogma: A Replication Study." *Entrepreneurship Theory and Practice* (2022). DOI: 10.1177/10422587211059991.

Binet, Les, and Peter Field. *The Long and the Short of It: Balancing Short and Long-Term Marketing Strategies*. London: Institute of Practitioners in Advertising, 2013.

BusinessBlogs. "The Man Who Destroyed his Multi-million Dollar Company in 10 Seconds." *BusinessBlogs.com*. Last updated 21 May 2022, https://www.businessblogshub.com/2012/09/the-man-who-destroyed-his-multi-million-dollar-company-in-10-seconds.

Caesar, Ed. "Not a Very Good Endorsement." *Independent*. Last modified 31 March 2005, https://www.independent.co.uk/news/media/not-a-very-good-endorsement-8592.html.

Campaign magazine. "APG Creative Strategy Awards – Comparethemarket.com 'meerkat campaign' by VCCP." *CampiagnLive*.co.uk. Last modified n.d., https://www.campaignlive.co.uk/article/apg-creative-strategy-awards-comparethemarketcom-meerkat-campaign-vccp/930643.

Choueke, Mark. "Swimming Against the Tide: Brands Need to Embrace a Culture of Creativity." *Marketing Week*. Last modified 4 January 2012, https://www.marketingweek.com/swimming-against-the-tide-brands-need-to-embrace-a-culture-of-creativity.

Dyson, James. *Invention: A Life*. London: Simon & Schuster UK, 2021.

Ebiquity. *The Challenge of Attention.* 2021. Accessed 3 September 2022, https://www.ebiquity.com/news-insights/viewpoints/the-challenge-of-attention.

Ehrenberg, A. (1969) "Towards an Integrated Theory of Consumer Behaviour." *Journal of the Market Research Society* 11 , no. 4 (1969).

Euro Effies. "Euro Effies Report." October 2016, https://issuu.com/eaca/docs/euro_effie_report_3c9b4615959540/1.

Field, Peter. "Brand Purpose: Is it Really All Misguided?" IPA Effworks. Last modified 25 October 2021, https://ipa.co.uk/knowledge/ipa-blog/brand-purpose-is-it-really-all-misguided.

Foster, Stephen. "Branding comes before advertising says new WPP study." *More About Advertising*. Last modified 27 May 2015, https://www.moreaboutadvertising.com/2015/05/branding-comes-before-advertising-says-new-wpp-study.

Hanssens, Dominique M. *Long-Term Impact of Marketing: A Compendium*. Singapore: World Scientific, 2018.

Jabr, Ferris. "Does Thinking Really Hard Burn More Calories?" *Scientific American*. Last modified 18 July 2012, https://www.scientificamerican.com/article/thinking-hard-calories.

Johannesson, Jokull. "The Ansoff Matrix revisited." Perren, L., Berry, A. and Clarke, I. (eds.) The End of the Pier? Competing Perspectives on the Challenges Facing Business and Management. London: British Academy of Management. 0954960858. pp. 15–21. Sept 2009.

Louis Vuitton. "Louis Vuitton and BMW i Partner to Create Luggage of the Future." Last modified 2 April 2022, https://uk.louisvuitton.com/eng-gb/articles/louis-vuitton-bmw-i-partner-to-create-luggage-of-the-future.

McLuhan, Marshall. *Understanding Media*. London: Routledge & Kegan Paul, 1964.

Mello, Toomy. "Jeff Bezos Used to Mock This Marketing Strategy, but He's Now Pouring Big Bucks Into It." Inc. Last modified 5 January 2021, https://www.inc.com/tommy-mello/jeff-bezos-used-to-mock-this-marketing-strategy-but-hes-now-pouring-big-bucks-into-it.html.

Mohammed, Shah. "Branding lessons – How did Intel build a brand around a commodity? – Ingredient Branding." *Medium*. Last modified 28 April 2017, https://shahmm.medium.com/branding-lessons-how-did-intel-build-a-brand-around-a-commodity-d48b29b71621.

Moore, Karl, and Susan Reid. "The Birth of Brand: 4000 Years of Branding History." *Business History* 4, no. 4 (2008): 419–432.

National Research Council. *Learning, Remembering, Believing: Enhancing Human Performance*. Washington, D.C.: National Academies Press, 1994.

Nielsen. "Global Trust in Advertising." Last modified September 2015, https://www.nielsen.com/insights/2015/global-trust-in-advertising-2015.

Pauwels, K., "Modeling Marketing Dynamics by Time Series Econometrics." *Marketing Letters*, 15, pp. 167-183 (2004).

Pymnts.com. "May The Star Wars Merch Be With You." Last modified 14 December 2019, https://www.pymnts.com/news/retail/2019/star-wars-disney-movie-merchandise-revenue.

ReferralCandy.com. "Word-of-Mouth: How Lush Cosmetics Hit Billion-dollar Revenues." Last modified 15 March 2019, https://www.referralcandy.com/blog/lush-word-of-mouth-marketing.

Romaniuk, Jenni. *Building Distinctive Brand Assets*. South Melbourne: Oxford University Press, 2018.

Schneider, Joan, and Julie Hall. "Why Most Product Launches Fail." *Harvard Business Review*. Last modified April 2011, https://hbr.org/2011/04/why-most-product-launches-fail.

Schrieber, Jared. "How to Grow Brands: Findings from 1 Billion Shopping Trips." MMA Global. Last modified 1 December 2021, https://www.mmaglobal.com/thegreatdebate/jared-schrieber-how-to-grow-brands.

Sharp, Byron. *How Brands Grow*. Melbourne: Oxford University Press, 2010.

Snyder, Jasper, and Manuel Garcia-Garcia. "Advertising across Platforms: Conditions for Multimedia Campaigns." *Journal of Advertising Research* 56, no. 4 (2016): 352-367.

Sook Known, Eun, Karen Whitehill King, Greg Nyilasy and Leonard N. Reid. "Impact of Media Context on Advertising Memory: A Meta-Analysis of Advertising Effectiveness." *Journal of Advertising Research*, 59, no. 1 (2018): 99-128.

The Branding Journal. "What to Learn From Tropicana's Packaging Redesign Failure?" Last modified 9 March 2022, https://www.thebrandingjournal.com/2015/05/what-to-learn-from-tropicanas-packaging-redesign-failure.

Tulving, Edel and W. Donaldson. "Episodic and semantic memory." *Organization of memory*. Academic Press (1972).

Vlaskovits, Patrick. "Henry Ford, Innovation, and that 'Faster Horse' Quote." *Harvard Business Review*. Last modified 29 August 2011, https://hbr.org/2011/08/henry-ford-never-said-the-fast.

Walsh, Coleen. "What the Nose Knows." *Harvard Gazette*. Last modified n.d., https://news.harvard.edu/gazette/story/2020/02/how-scent-emotion-and-memory-are-intertwined-and-exploited.

White, Dan. *The Smart Marketing Book: The Definitive Guide to Effective Marketing Strategies*. London: LID Publishing, 2020.

Zappos website. "20 Years, 20 Milestones: How Zappos Grew Out Of Just Shoes." Last modified n.d., https://www.zappos.com/about/stories/zappos-20th-birthday.

World Heritage Encyclopaedia. "Sex in Advertising." Last modified n.d., http://worldheritage.org/articles/eng/Sex_in_advertising.

ACKNOWLEDGEMENTS

Many thanks to Alex White, Sophie Neiman and Graham Staplehurst for their help and advice.

ABOUT THE AUTHOR

DAN WHITE is a marketing and insights innovator. His career includes a decade as an insights professional, another as a brand advisor and a third as a Chief Marketing Officer.

Dan co-developed BRANDZ, the world's biggest brand equity measurement system and his thinking has shaped the design of leading copy test and brand tracking methodologies. As a brand and communications guru, he has advised famous, billion-dollar brands on how to thrive and his summaries and trademark visualizations have earned praise from luminaries in the marketing, advertising, and media industries.

Every sentence and every hand-drawn illustration in *The Smart Branding Book* has been crafted to ensure readers can understand and apply the often-complex concepts needed to make smart branding choices.

FROM THE SAME AUTHOR

The Smart Marketing Book
LID Publishing, 2020

The Soft Skills Book
LID Publishing, 2021